D0314934

kamera
B O O K S

www.kamerabooks.co.uk

David Carter

THE WESTERN

kamera
BOOKS

First published in 2008 by Kamera Books
PO Box 394, Harpenden, Herts, AL5 1XJ
www.kamerabooks.com

Copyright © David Carter, 2008
Series Editor: Hannah Patterson

A CIP catalogue record for this book is available from the British Library.

ISBN-10: 1-84243-217-6
ISBN-13: 978-1-84243-217-4

Typeset by Avocet Typeset, Chilton, Aylesbury, Bucks
Printed by SNP Lefung Printers (Shenzen) Co Ltd, China

In memory cf my father and mother,
Joseph and Elizabeth Carter,
who took me to see my first 'cowboy films'.

ACKNOWLEDGEMENTS

My greatest debt in writing this book is to all the fans I have discussed westerns with over the years, to the major scholars in the field, and to my ever-diligent editor Hannah Patterson.

CONTENTS

INTRODUCTION

In one sense, 'The Western' hardly needs an introduction. In the two decades prior to World War Two, and in the first three after it in particular, most cinemagoers could describe the main characteristics of a western: stories of rugged people in harsh terrains, attempting to settle and civilise the western territories of America; their conflicts with the Native Americans known as Indians; their struggles to establish law and order; wagon trains, stagecoaches and newly built railroads; sheriffs and marshals battling against outlaws; gold rushes and bank robberies; shoot-outs and hangings; buffalo stampedes, cattle drives and rustlers. Nowadays, there are a vast number of academic books and encyclopaedic volumes devoted to the genre, and a book of the present scope cannot and does not attempt to compete with them. Some of the most useful of the more extensive studies are listed in the resources section together with some relevant general works of reference. What this book does aim to provide is a general introduction for the enthusiast or student who wishes to discover more about the range and variety of western films, and also a source of reference for both the recognised classics of the genre and some that have been unjustly neglected or overlooked.

Aside from a chapter devoted to Italian westerns (the so-called 'spaghetti westerns'), the book's main focus is the American cinema western. Although a considerable number of westerns have been made outside America, not only in Italy and Spain but also in countries such as Germany and Russia – to date 500 at least – space here does not permit a survey of these. Neither is there scope to explore the close links that have existed between cinema westerns and TV series, but several of the books mentioned in the resources section do provide further information.

The Western does, however, cover the historical background of the American West, and also westerns in literature, which predated and greatly influenced many of the great cinema westerns. Information is also provided on the notable historical events which westerns either alluded to or recreated, usually distorting and romanticising the facts.

Emphasis is placed on the so-called 'Golden Age' (from the late 30s to the 70s approximately), when many recognised classic westerns were produced, a choice that reflects the declining popularity of the genre as a whole. Other chapters consider more recent contributions to the genre and modern classic westerns.

Ironically, while the early silent period was the most prolific in terms of the number of films made, with many hundreds being made in many years, most were very short, cheaply made and of little artistic merit. Only the outstanding achievements of this period are examined here. Many low-budget films, known as 'B' westerns, were also made during the 1940s and 50s. A brief mention of them is made in chapter 5.

Most westerns do not fit into easy compartments and for any complex and thorough consideration would have to be considered under several headings at least: westerns about revenge, westerns about law and order, feminist westerns, revisionist westerns and so on. One of the most impressive scholarly studies of the western – David Lusted's 'The Western' – manages this feat and it is an excellent and extensive study. However, it requires prior knowledge of a large number of westerns to be appreciated fully. Since many readers will come to the present book knowing maybe a reasonable number of westerns, some of the major directors in the genre, and the most well-known actors, the films in chapter 5, about the 'Golden Age', are organised by the director's name. After a brief biography, the major westerns of each director are listed chronologically, with only the screenplay writers acknowledged each time. Actors, cinematographers, etc are mentioned where relevant in the plot summaries or comments. Other headings such as 'Music' are introduced occasionally if they are of particular importance in the film. Some other works which do not fit easily into the lists of major directors but are worthy of attention are included in chapter 7, and organised chronologically with the same range of credits. There are special sections on 'Comic Westerns' (chapter 8) and the most well-known 'spaghetti westerns' (chapter 9). Chapter 10, entitled 'The Death and Rebirth of the Western', provides similar information and comments on some recent westerns. In addition, some recognised classics mentioned in chapters 5 and 10 are accorded more extensive analysis in chapters 6 and 11 respectively.

It must be stressed that many films could fit well into several different chapters. This is especially true of some of the comedy westerns in chapter 8. The easiest way to find entries on particular films is therefore to refer to its title or director's name in the Index.

Finally, one matter should be clarified concerning the issue of political correctness. Throughout the book I have quite deliberately used the term 'Indians' for the peoples who are nowadays referred to as 'Native Americans'. This is because it was the term commonly used in the nineteenth century and in virtually all the westerns in which they appear. It would be pedantic and historically unjustified to use the more recent terminology. The reader should therefore assume that whenever the term 'Indian/s' occurs, the concept of 'Native American' is implied.

THE HISTORICAL SETTING

THE WEST

The concept of 'The West' is a very loosely defined term, both geographically and historically, when applied to those parts of America associated with the literary and film genre of 'The Western'. Apart from the eastern seaboard, almost every part of the United States had been referred to as 'The West' at some stage in the country's history. Nowadays most people take it to refer to the area of the Great Plains and the Southwest in general, but officially the federal government defines 'The West' as including the following states: Alaska, Arizona, California, Hawaii, Idaho, Montana, Nevada, New Mexico, Oregon, Utah, Washington and Wyoming. 'The West' referred to in popular imagination, in literature and film consists usually of those areas associated with the final frontiers of American settlement, incorporating specifically the plains, mountains and deserts to the west of the Mississippi River. This is the area associated commonly with cowboys, Indians, covered wagons and outlaws. But cowboys and cattle driving were also common in several non-western states, such as Nebraska and Kansas.

Most of this western area became part of the United States through the Louisiana Purchase in 1803, though the Southwest remained a Mexican possession until 1848. The Pacific Northwest was opened up for settlement via the Oregon Trail, which was established by the Lewis and Clark Expedition of 1804–06. Crucial in increasing migration to the West Coast was the discovery of gold in California in 1848. This led to the admission of California into the Union in 1850, only two years after it had been ceded from Mexico.

The Great Plains remained only sparsely populated for many decades, thought of as inhospitable desert land, with little water, and hostile Indian tribes. By and large, they were not opened up to white settlement until after the Civil War of 1861–65, when the Plains Indians were gradually conquered and eventually deprived of most of their lands by the settlers and through the agency of the US Cavalry. The conflicts between the white pioneers and the Indian tribes in these areas formed one of the basic themes in the western genre. Another central theme became the conflicts between the Indians and the cowboys, hired by ranchers to drive cattle across many hundreds of miles to railheads where the animals could be transported east to the markets. With the development of cattle-farming and mining communities also came the growth of towns, many of them with rather unruly lifestyles. Imposing some system of law and order became a major concern in many such places, and another major theme in many westerns, with the figures of the town sheriff, his posse of honest men, and US marshals featuring prominently.

By circa 1870 only a few parts of the Great Plains could be truly described as unsettled. And by the late 1880s, as the great cattle ranges declined in importance, large areas were fenced off into family farms. And with this, together with the settlement of the Oklahoma Indian Territory, the last period of large-scale westward migration came to an end. By the early 1890s no real western frontier existed anymore.

THE REPUBLIC OF TEXAS AND THE ALAMO

Texas played a special role in the history of the American West and made its own unique contributions to the mythology of the western. Following the coup in Mexico in 1833, when Antonio Lopez de Santa Anna took over the presidency, many Texans supported him in the hope that this would strengthen their own chances of gaining freedom from restrictive government control. Santa Anna, however, considered the Texans to be fermenting insurrection. It came to outright conflict when the Texans first set up their own provisional government in 1835, and then in 1336 declared independence. David G Burnett became the new interim president of the Republic of Texas and Sam Houston its military commander. It was not simply a conflict between Anglo-American settlers and Mexican soldiers. Many of the revolutionaries were themselves Mexicans, who supported the same goal as the white Texans: freedom from tyranny.

One famous event during the ten-year life of the republic was to find many literary and cinematic treatments: the siege of the Alamo. The siege of the Alamo, a group of former Franciscan chapel buildings in San Antonio, lasted from February 23 to March 6, 1836. The aim of the confrontation between the Texan settlers in the fort and the attacking Mexican forces was to keep off the Mexican troops long enough to enable the Texans to organise themselves militarily. The climax of the siege involved a massive attack by the Mexicans, resulting in all the defenders, apart from a few women and children, being killed, including two men who were to become legendary: Jim Bowie and Davy Crockett. The Texans secured victory over the Mexicans on April 21, however, when Sam Houston led a surprise attack on the Mexicans at the San Jacinto River, where he also managed to capture their leader Santa Anna. The Alamo, which has been restored as a historic site, has become an important symbol of Texan identity.

During the ten-year life of the republic there were frequent raids by Mexicans and also Indians. To combat these incursions a mobile, armed force was founded which also became a stock western theme: the Texas Rangers.

THE CIVIL WAR

The American Civil War (1861–65) was between the federal government of the United States and eleven southern states who wanted to secede from the Union. The states in question were South Carolina, North Carolina, Florida, Alabama, Louisiana, Virginia, Arkansas, Mississippi, Tennessee, Texas and Georgia. Apart from issues of trade and tariffs, the primary concerns were the states' own rights and the question of slavery. The northern states mainly depended on the manufacturing industries and small farms, while the southern economy was mainly dependent on slave labour on the large cotton plantations. By the 1850s many northerners were demanding the abolition of slavery, and the southern states threatened to secede to protect their social and economic structure. With the election of Abraham Lincoln to the presidency as the candidate of the Republican Party, which was strongly against slavery, the southern states carried out their threat to secede.

After several years of conflict Lincoln gave supreme command of the army to General Ulysses S Grant, in March 1864. By March 1885, the southern army under General Robert E Lee was in a desperate situation: low on supplies, with countless casualties, having lost many troops through desertion. Lee surrendered on April 3 and by the end of the month the war was over. The victory by the North ensured the preservation of the Union and brought about the abolition of slavery, granting citizenship to the freed slaves.

NATIVE AMERICANS

THE PLAINS INDIANS

When people think of the Indians of North America it is usually those of the Great Plains. They occupied an extensive area between the Mississippi River and the Rocky Mountains, including parts of Canada as well as the United States. It consists predominantly of broad grasslands stretching from Saskatchewan, Alberta and Manitoba in the north to the border of Texas along the Rio Grande in the south. All the tribes in this area were mainly hunters of wild game, especially buffalo, which provided not only their main source of food but also materials for shelter, clothing and various tools. The most well-known of the tribes, or nations, mainly due to their prominence in the western genre, are the Sioux (also known as the Dakota), the Cheyenne, and the Pawnee. Other well-known names are the Cree, the Blackfoot, the Crow, and the Arapaho. As well as having their own distinctive languages, the Indians also used a standardised sign language for communication between tribes speaking different languages. It involved a system of fixed hand and finger positions symbolising ideas. These feature in some western films, though often in crude form.

THE SOUTHWEST INDIANS

The other major area of Native American habitation is that within, and bordering, Arizona and New Mexico. It is a very dry and climatically unstable region between the Rocky Mountains and the Sierra Madre in Mexico. The Indian tribes living in this area had to adopt lifestyles which enabled them to cope with often unfavourable geographical conditions. They became extremely diversified culturally and linguistically, but can be identified in roughly four groups: the Yuman tribes constituting the first, the Pima and the Papago the second, the more widely known Pueblo Indians (meaning 'Village-dwelling' Indians) making up the third group, and probably the most famous, the Navajo and Apache, the fourth.

NOTABLE HISTORICAL EVENTS

The Battle of the Little Bighorn

The Second Treaty of Fort Laramie, in 1868, guaranteed to the Eastern Sioux (Dakota) and Northern Cheyenne Indians exclusive possession of the Dakota territory west of the Missouri River, but white miners in search of gold started settling on land which the Indians regarded as sacred. The US government was unwilling to remove the settlers and could not persuade the Indians to sell the territory. When the Indians started attacking the settlers in the territory, the government felt that this released them from the obligations of the treaty and ordered them to return to their reservations, otherwise appropriate action would be taken. In June 1876, the government sent in troops under the command of Brigadeer General Alfred H Terry to drive the Indians from the territory. It was planned to trap the Indians between two groups of government troops, one led by Terry, the other by Lieutenant Colonel George A Custer with the 7th Cavalry. Custer abandoned the agreed plan and pursued a strategy of his own. A large force of Indians eventually managed to attack Custer and his men, leaving more than 200 dead including Custer. This event so stunned the white Americans that large numbers of forces were sent in to force the Indians into a final surrender. This battle, which took place near the Little Bighorn River, has also become known as 'Custer's Last Stand'. It has been much discussed and analysed, and featured in many a western film, for example *The Great Sioux Massacre* (1965), directed by Sydney Salkow, and *Custer of the West* (1967), directed by Robert Siodmak.

The Battle of Wounded Knee

In the late 1880s the Teton Sioux Indians decided to follow the advice of one of their prophets, who promised that white men would leave their country and they would regain their herds of buffalo if they performed certain traditional rites and dances, known as the Ghost Dance. The American federal army became anxious about this activity and suppressed it. The famous Indian leader Chief Sitting Bull was killed while being arrested. Several hundred Sioux then left the reservation and gathered around another leader, Chief Big Foot. As they had left their reservation the American military regarded them as hostile. The Indians were surrounded and they surrendered without conflict at their encampment near the hamlet and creek known as Wounded Knee on the Pine Ridge Indian Reservation in southwest South Dakota.

Unfortunately an incident involving violence led to a massacre. One young Indian was reluctant to give up his new rifle and in the ensuing scuffle a soldier was shot. The soldiers panicked and fired at the Indians from close range with their machine guns. The Indians only had their clubs and knives to defend themselves. Though many of the Indians attempted to escape they were hunted down and killed. It is not known exactly how many Indians were killed as the Indians later removed some of their dead, but 144 Indians, including 44 women and 16 children, were eventually buried in a mass grave. 30 American soldiers died.

The event and the site at Wounded Knee became a symbol for Native American identity and nationhood. On February 27, 1973, about 200 members of the American Indian Movement took the hamlet of Wounded Knee by force and declared it the 'Independent Oglala Sioux Nation'. They vowed that they would stay there until the US government met their aim of agreeing to a general review of Indian grievances in general. The Indians were surrounded by federal marshals and a siege ensued involving the deaths of two Indians and the serious wounding of one marshal. Finally the Indians surrendered when the government agreed to set up negotiations to address their grievances.

The Johnson County War

In April 1892 a range war took place in Johnson County, Wyoming, around which many legends and myths have grown up. Numerous stories, novels and films have used events of this war or the general setting of this war as the background for fictional events. Johnson County was not the only scene of such conflicts, but it is the one most remembered. In fact conflicts about the ownership of land became especially prevalent in the late 1800s and early 1900s. It had been common practice to allow free grazing on most of the land or open range in Wyoming. Cattle rustling became widespread, often through surreptitious branding of cattle on the open range. The owners of large ranches often resorted to violence to defend their cattle, and organised themselves into associations to monopolise large areas of land and prevent any new settlers in the area. The conflicts became acute after the poor winter of 1887–88, when many cattle were lost, and the powerful landowners employed gunmen to kill alleged rustlers, though often innocent people died as a result and illegal lynchings were common. It came to an all-out local war when one of the major organisations of landowners, the WSGA (the Wyoming Stock Growers Association), hired a number of gunmen from Texas, who organised a group of 50 men to eliminate the rustlers once and for all and destroy an organised group of farmers with small holdings who had banded together under the name of the Northern Wyoming Farmers and Stock Growers Association (NWFSGA). It was these events that have provided the background to many films about range wars, cattle rustling and illegal lynchings, most notably *Shane* (1953) and *Heaven's Gate* (1980).

THE WESTERN IN LITERATURE

Literary treatments of themes and events related to settlement of the western territories, albeit in crude and sensationalist forms, date back to the early exploits of the pioneers before the Civil War. The lives of trappers, buffalo hunters and scouts proved to be endlessly fascinating to those living in more secure circumstances in the East. The earliest works of this genre of undoubted artistic worth are those of James Fennimore Cooper, notably *The Pioneers* (1823), *The Last of the Mohicans* (1826) and *The Prairie* (1827), but these works were not really typical of the many more popular narratives which were to follow. The most famous of them, *The Last of the Mohicans*, reflects the conflicts of the British colonial forces with Native Americans, whereas the vast majority of westerns are set clearly in independent America. An early populariser of western stories wrote under the pseudonym Ned Buntline (EZC Judson) and produced large numbers of cheap yarns, gaining himself the nickname 'father of the dime novel'. He also became renowned for turning the real-life Buffalo Bill into a figure of mythic proportions.

The first novel with the classic Western characteristics and settings to gain true critical acclaim was *The Virginian* (1902) by Owen Wister. Wister actually visited the West, where he gained his inspiration for the work, while recuperating from an illness. Two men who worked as cowboys wrote popular books based on their experiences: Andy Adams used his own experience as the basis of *Log of a Cowboy* (1903) and Eugene Manlove Rhodes, who had been both cowboy and scout, wrote

Bransford in Arcadia (1914), which was reprinted in 1917 as *Bransford of Rainbow Range*.

Many writers of novels also produced short stories in the western genre. Stephen Crane wrote a memorable comic western story called *The Bride Comes to Yellow Sky* (1898) and AH Lewis (circa 1858–1914), who was a former cowboy, wrote a series of purportedly true stories told by a character called the 'Old Cattleman'. Other notable western writers were WM Raine (1871–1954), who wrote more than 80 western novels, Conrad Richter (1890–1968) and Ernest Haycox (1899–1950). Hamlin Gareland's *Son of the Middle Border* (1917) and OE Rölvaag's *Giants in the Earth* (1927) were also popular. Emerson Hough's *Covered Wagon* (1922) was the basis of a very influential silent film with the same title made in the following year. One woman writer, BM Bower (1871–1940), wrote so convincingly that she was believed by many to be a man. Two of the most prolific and most popular western writers, who have retained a following to the present day, are Louis L'Amour and Zane Grey, whose most famous work is *Riders of the Purple Sage* (1912).

Some mention should be made of the German writer Karl May who popularised the genre in Europe with tales about North American Indians. His stories first appeared in the early 1890s, and altogether he produced more than 60 works. His most famous characters were 'Old Shatterhand' and 'Winnetou'. As late as the 1960s and 1970s his novels and their film adaptations still had a strong following in Germany.

Western novels of undoubted literary merit are *The Ox-Bow Incident* (1940), about a lynching in Nevada, by Walter van Tilburg Clark, *The Big Sky* (1947), about frontier life back in the 1840s, by AB Guthrie, and *Shane* (1949) by Jack Schaefer, all of which were turned into successful films. Another well-known work by Guthrie is *The Way West* (1949). The novel *Lonesome Dove* (1985), by Larry McMurtry, is also worthy of note.

The peak of interest in western novels was undoubtedly in the 1950s and the early 1960s, when there were also a large number of television western series. Ray Hogan, Luke Short, Lash La Rue and Louis L'Amour were in their heyday at that time. Since the 1970s and 1980s, apart from the works of a few cult authors, such as Louis L'Amour and George G Gilman, the western can no longer be said to be a popular genre, though Cormac McCarthy, author of *All the Pretty Horses* (made into a film directed by Billy Bob Thornton and released in 2000), is acquiring a dedicated following.

THE SILENT WESTERNS

Hundreds upon hundreds of silent films in the western genre were made, most of which have been lost to posterity. Certain directors and actors, however, stand out for their achievements and influence on the future course of the genre.

Most studies of the western film are agreed about the first major film of the genre, but to be historically accurate it must be noted that there s a record of at least one very short western before the end of the nineteenth century: *Cripple Creek Barroom* (1898). The first truly commercial success was *The Great Train Robbery* (1903), directed by Edwin S Porter, which was followed by a direct remake the following year by another company and a wave of close imitations. The production company for the original film, Edison, finally made a parody of its own f lm, *The Little Train Robbery*, in 1905. In 1906 another Edison western, *A Race for Millions*, included a street gunfight, which would become a cliché of the genre.

One of the most well-known and influential directors of the silent era, DW Griffith, also made a series of successful westerns in the period before the First World War. Among the many a few are worthy of note. In 1911 appeared his *Fighting Blood*, set in the period after the Civil War and starring Lionel Barrymore, and in the same year *The Last Drop of Water*. 1912 saw the release of *Goddess of Sagebrush Gulch*, set in a California mining town. In the same year he made *The Massacre* (released in 1914), based on the Battle of the Little Bighorn, and in 1913 *Scarlet Days*. In 1914 there followed *Battle at Elderbush Gulch*, featuring

Lionel Barrymore once again and Lillian Gish. After this Griffith made no more westerns.

Producers soon discovered that audiences were attracted by star heroes, and the first of the kind was GM Anderson, who established the character of Broncho Billy, a Robin Hood figure who was basically good at heart. Very few of his 500-odd short films have survived. Two other significant stars of silent westerns were William S Hart and Tom Mix.

The advent of sound in the late 1920s was a major challenge to the western genre, because at first sound films had to be made in special studios, and the western had come to rely on many outdoor sequences involving chases and gunfights. Directors initially reduced the number of such sequences until they discovered ways to record natural outdoor soundtracks.

SILENT WESTERN STARS

'BRONCHO BILLY' (GM ANDERSON)

Before he became famous as a director and actor, GM Anderson worked more on the business side of film production. His first highly successful film as an actor was *The Bandit Makes Good* (1907). He claimed that he only played the lead of 'Broncho Billy' because he could not find any other suitable actor to play the part. Anderson did not regard this as part of the subsequent 'Broncho Billy' series, however, the first of which he claimed was *Broncho Billy and the Baby* (1908), about an outlaw who relinquishes his freedom to help a lost child. As 'Broncho Billy', Anderson starred in 100s of short westerns, making more than 375 of them between 1908 and 1915, some with rather unlikely titles, such as *Broncho Billy's Christmas Dinner* (1911), and *Broncho Billy's Bible* (1914). In 1957 he was awarded an Oscar® for his contribution to the development of entertainment films.

WILLIAM S HART

The notion of the bad man with a heart of gold may have been introduced into the western film by GM Anderson, but William S Hart developed it more fully in his screen persona over more than 50 westerns. After working for some time as a stage actor he first appeared in a feature film in 1914 as the outlaw in *The Bargain*, directed by Reginald Barker. The outlaw is injured while robbing a stagecoach and looked after by a rancher's daughter, with whom he falls in love. Both this and *On the Night Stage* (1915) became very popular. Other notable films by Hart are *The Disciple* (1915) and *The Narrow Trail* (1917). Many of the films he co-directed. His own favourite was *The Aryan* (1915) in which a gold prospector (Hart) is relieved of his riches by members of a small township. He is consumed by thoughts of revenge and kidnaps one of the women in the town. It seems he has lost all ability to sympathise with the plights of others until he develops some affection for a young girl. *Hell's Hinges* (1916), in which a gunman (Hart) is hired by a gambler to stop the local priest's efforts at reform, but the gunman is captivated by the priest's sister and turns to reading the Bible, is another of his films which is greatly admired.

In 1923 he appeared in a worthy version of the exploits of a famous historical figure: *Wild Bill Hickok*, directed by Clifford S Smith. Hickok (Hart) arrives in Dodge City where he divides his time between gambling and helping maintain some semblance of law and order. The main focus of the action is his pursuit of an escaped outlaw, whom he eventually guns down. He decides to leave town, however, when he discovers he is falling in love with a married woman. The film is fairly faithful to historical reality, and includes a reference to the fact that Hickok was slowly going blind. Hart's last film, *Tumbleweeds* (1925), has been greatly admired for its cinematography (Joseph H August) and Hart's own performance. Here he plays a ranch owner who, together with the woman he loves, plan to stake a claim to land when it is made available to settlers in the Oklahoma Territory.

TOM MIX

Tom Mix was certainly the most popular star in silent westerns, though his style was very different to that of William S Hart. Mix went in for rather flashy costumes and preferred a romantic, escapist view of the West. Whereas Hart had his roots in the theatre, Mix was basically a showman, proud of his skills as a horseman and frequently appearing in rodeos. His first role was in *Ranch Life in the Great Southwest* (1910), and he appeared in several films until he joined the Fox company in 1917, when his career as a charismatic cowboy took off. The first film to make him truly famous was *The Untamed* (1920). In *Just Tony* (1922) he plays a cowboy seeking revenge against a man who shot him. Without realising it he falls in love with the man's daughter. In the course of the action he finds a horse, called Tony, who stays with him as his faithful companion through subsequent films. Other Mix films that were particularly popular were *The Lone Star Ranger* (1923), *Riders of the Purple Sage* (1925), based on the 1912 story by Zane Grey, and *The Great K & A Train Robbery* (1926). In the latter film Mix saves a girl from an accident, and she turns out to be the daughter of the president of the K & A Railroad. He discovers that the male secretary of the company, who is also interested in the president's daughter, is selling company secrets to bandits planning to rob the company. Needless to say the film culminates with Mix routing the bandits.

Mix continued to have some success in the sound era, and in 1932 he appeared in one of three famous versions of a novel by Max Brand, *Destry Rides Again*. It does not follow the book closely, but was very popular with audiences. He died in a car accident in 1940.

SILENT WESTERN CLASSICS

The Great Train Robbery (1903)

B&W. 12 mins.
Directed by: Edwin S Porter
Written by: Edwin S Porter

Plot: Four masked men force a telegraph operator at a station to send a message which will cause a train to make an unscheduled stop. They attack the train and rob the mail van. One of the passengers is killed while trying to escape. A message gets through to the sheriff who rounds up a posse and pursues the bandits, resulting in a shootout.

Comments: Maintaining a strong narrative line throughout, one famous shot, included various y at the start or the end of the film, shows a bandit firing directly at the camera, thus engaging the audience emotionally in the action.

Fighting Blood (1911)

B&W. 18 mins.
Directed by: DW Griffith

Plot: The film is set in the Dakota Territory after the Civil War, where an ex-soldier and his family have settled. After a quarrel the son leaves home, but encounters a band of Indians attacking the home of a neighbour. Hotly pursued by the Indians the son hurries home to warn his family.

Comments: Justly praised for its insight into human behaviour, all crammed into a mere 18 minutes.

The Last Drop of Water (1911)

B&W. One reel.
Directed by: DW Griffith
Written by: DW Griffith

Plot: The film follows the troubles which beset a wagon train heading westward, including the love lives of some of the members.

Comments: Considered to be an important influence on James Cruze's *The Covered Wagon* (1923).

Battle at Elderbush Gulch (1914)

B&W. 29 mins.
Directed by: DW Griffith
Written by: DW Griffith

Plot: A young mother (Lillian Gish) travels west by stagecoach with her husband and baby. A tribe of Indians become drunk and steal the settlers' pet dogs which they want to use as food. When the white men kill the Indian chief's son, the Indians attack the settlers, and the lives of the woman, her child and a young homeless girl are in danger.

Comments: Griffith employed a technique, which would later become cliché, of intercutting shots from sequences of parallel action to increase tension. Here shots of the Indians attacking are intercut with ones of cavalry hurrying to the rescue. The film has been criticised for its racist depiction of the Indians as drunken savages, while the whites appear as representatives of ideal family values.

The Covered Wagon (1923)

B&W. 98 mins
Directed by: James Cruze
Written by: Jack Cunningham

Plot: Set in 1848, the film follows the adventures of a covered wagon train that is cut off from the main convoy on its way to Oregon. The travellers decide to head instead for California in search of gold.

Comments: Based on Emerson Hough's story of the same name, the film is considered by many nowadays to be overly sentimental. Efforts were made to achieve some historical authenticity, however, and the director's own grandfather had experience of such journeys. Whatever its limitations by today's standards, it can be truly described as the first epic western, combining a sense of space and distance with a concern for realism.

The Iron Horse (1924)

B&W. 133 mins.
Directed by: John Ford
Written by: Charles Darnton and Charles Kenyon

Plot: The story of the building of the transcontinental railroad, it traces the process from initial planning (including a meeting with Abraham Lincoln) through the construction process, to the final meeting of the two railheads in Utah. Interwoven is the story of two childhood friends, Davy and Miriam, who are parted when Davy's father takes him with him out west. Davy's father is murdered by Indians led by a white man. Later Miriam becomes engaged to a surveyor with one of the companies building the railroad. A powerful landowner called Bauman, who tries to arrange by devious means for the railroad to run through his property, is finally revealed to be the man who murdered Davy's father.

Comments: The director John Ford had already made about 40 westerns before this, which was shot almost entirely on location under severe conditions. Featuring smooth camerawork and well-edited climaxes, it also contains features which were to become hallmarks of Ford westerns: the combination of historical narrative with personal drama, evocative landscapes, and the use of comic interludes (here a group of Irish labourers).

The Winning of Barbara Worth (1926)

B&W. 8 reels.
Directed by: Henry King
Written by: Frances Marion

Plot: A man finds an orphan girl in the desert and raises her as his own daughter, Barbara Worth. When she grows up she is loved by the foreman of her father's ranch (played by Gary Cooper). An irrigation engineer from the east (played by Ronald Colman) also falls in love with her and an intense rivalry develops. The foreman discovers that the financier, who is a partner of Barbara's father in a dam-building project, plans to deceive his partners. The foreman overcomes his animosity towards the engineer and warns him of the imminent collapse of the dam. Tragedy ensues.

Comments: The film was a big hit but is mainly remembered today for the performances of Gary Cooper (in his first major role) and Ronald Colman, both of whom were to go on to be leading stars in Hollywood.

THE GOLDEN AGE OF WESTERNS: FROM HEYDAY TO MATURITY

During the 1940s and 1950s, the western as a genre took off, becoming big box office and featuring the major stars of the day, some of whom, such as Randolph Scott, Joel McCrea, John Wayne and Gary Cooper, specialised in westerns above all other types of film. Though they may have played a range of roles in different film genres, it is for their performances in westerns that they are mainly remembered. Other major actors too contributed memorable performances in the genre: Alan Ladd, Glenn Ford, James Garner, Henry Fonda, Jack Palance, Dale Robertson and Robert Ryan, not to mention the actor who was later to be president, Ronald Reagan. Countless other leading Hollywood stars featured prominently in westerns at some time in their careers, including leading ladies such as Joan Crawford, Jane Russell, Maureen O'Hara, to mention a mere few. Then there were those stalwarts who provided colourful support to the main stars with a rich range of often eccentric performances in what became known as 'character' roles: Victor McLaglen, Walter Brennan, Warren Oates, Dan Duryea and the inimitable George 'Gabby' Hayes, amongst others.

While changes took place in the character of western films over the next few decades – and these will be traced as they reveal themselves – it is increasingly difficult to break the films down into categories or types. It is certainly true that in the best films there was a progressive complexity in the depiction of moral issues, character, motivation, the plight of the Native American Indians, the role of women, and the issues of law and order. Some critics have attempted to distinguish between what might be termed the 'heyday' of the western, in the 1940s and 1950s, when it was certainly at the height of its popularity, and the later years of the 'mature epics' in the 1960s and 1970s. It has been argued that the westerns produced in the first decade after the Second World War in particular often deal with more controversial themes. By the later 1960s especially, the treatment of Native American Indians by the whites was presented more critically, and violence and sexuality not only became central themes but they were more graphically depicted. That said, this was true of films in all genres at the time.

From the 1940s on, not only had stars dominated the public interest but certain directors were considered as authors of their own works, developing a coherent body of films reflecting a general philosophy of life (the 'auteur' concept of filmmaking). It therefore makes for a more coherent representation of the development of the western in this so-called 'Golden Age' to analyse it by the output of its main directors, not in the entirety of that output, but through consideration of their major works within the western genre.

First, though, some tribute must be paid to those actors and crews who produced good quality entertainment films, known as 'B' westerns, which often filled up the second part of a double bill during the 1940s and 1950s. Many hundreds of them were produced in any one year during those decades. Most are lost or no longer readily available. Many of their leading actors made entire careers as stars of 'B' westerns, such as Johnny Mack Brown. Two actors in 'B' westerns became famous, went on to make some memorable features and live on in the popular imagination: William Boyd, with his character of Hopalong Cassidy, and Roy Rogers. There is unfortunately insufficient room within the scope of the present book to analyse this aspect of the genre. Some guidelines for further study are supplied in the books listed in the section on resources.

THE MAJOR DIRECTORS AND THEIR FILMS

Not all directors of westerns are considered here, but only those who contributed significantly to the genre, by their extensive output, quality of filmmaking or influence. The lists are alphabetical according to director's family name, with dates. This is followed by a brief biography and useful additional information. The films are listed chronologically. A few westerns made in the 1930s are also included if they are generally considered to be important works, although this section is primarily concerned with the development of the western from the 1940s onwards. One film from 1928 is included under Raoul Walsh, and in a few cases some films from recent decades have been included, to provide an overview of the director's output in the genre. Some of the films are also considered later in this book, in which case a reference to the relevant chapter is included. Films in black and white are designated thus: B&W. All others are in colour.

ROBERT ALDRICH

b. 1918. d. 1983.

Aldrich joined RKO Pictures in 1941 as a production clerk, and worked his way up to production manager and associate producer. In the 1950s he wrote and directed TV series. His first feature film was *Big Leaguer* (1953). He eventually set up his own production company, and among his best-known films as director are *The Flight of the Phoenix* (1965), the thriller *Whatever Happened to Baby Jane?* (1962), and the Second World War drama *The Dirty Dozen* (1967). Of his westerns the most well known are the two released in 1954: *Apache* and *Vera Cruz*.

Apache (1954)

Written by: James R Webb

Plot: Massai (Burt Lancaster) is the 'last Apache', in terms of a fighting warrior. After the surrender of Geronimo (Monte Blue), he is captured. He manages to escape and tries to make his way back to his homeland and rejoin his wife (Jean Peters). He attempts to fight single-handedly against the US Cavalry, but is finally forced to surrender.

Comments: The studio forced Aldrich to change his original ending, which would have presented the US army in a negative light: shooting Massai in the back and killing him. Burt Lancaster turned in one of his particularly heavy performances in a film which is interesting for its attempt to show that not all Indians believed unequivocally that they should fight against the white men in order to preserve their traditional ways of life. Some followed the principle that the only way to survive was to imitate the white men's ways.

Vera Cruz (1954)

Written by: Roland Kibbee and James R Webb

Plot: Two American mercenaries, Trane (Gary Cooper) and Erin (Burt Lancaster), fight together during the Mexican revolution. A peasant girl, Nina (Sarita Montiel), wants them to fight on the side of the peasants but the Marquis de Labordere (Cesar Romero) wants them to fight for the Emperor Maximilian. The countess Marie Duvarre (Denise Darcel) persuades them to escort her to Vera Cruz. She eventually reveals that her real purpose is to take a shipment of gold to the Emperor's army.

Comments: Despite its rather convoluted plot and the unprincipled behaviour of almost everyone concerned, the film was a great success at the box office, doubtless because it featured two famous stars together. The cinematography by Ernest Laszlo alone makes it worth viewing.

The Last Sunset (1961)

Written by: Dalton Trumbo

Plot: Sheriff Dana Stribling (Rock Hudson) is pursuing the outlaw Brendan 'Bren' O'Malley (Kirk Douglas), who has killed his brother-in-law. O'Malley eventually rejoins an ex-lover Belle Breckenridge (Dorothy Malone) and is now attracted to her daughter Melissa (Carol Lynley). Stribling finds himself falling for Belle, and Belle reveals that Melissa is actually O'Malley's own daughter. The film culminates in a shoot-out between Stribling and O'Malley.

Comments: Featuring characters that are complex and darkly motivated, the film touches on the sensitive subject of incestuous desire. Its title suggests the end of an era and way of life.

4 for Texas (1963)

Written by: Robert Aldrich

Plot: Zack Thomas (Frank Sinatra) and Joe Jarrett (Dean Martin) compete with each other to control a town's casinos. They eventually have to support each other in the interest of destroying a ruthless banker, Harvey Burden (Victor Buono), and his henchman Matson (Charles Bronson).

Comments: Love interest (it is more a matter of titillation) is provided by Elya (Anita Ekberg) and Maxine (Ursula Andress). Displays of cleavage seem to have loomed larger among the producers' priorities than acting skills. The film provides fairly harmless fun but little more.

Ulzana's Raid (1972)

Written by: Alan Sharp

Plot: An Indian fighter, Ulzana (Joaquin Martinez), is terrorising the settlers in Arizona. McIntosh (Burt Lancaster), a veteran army scout, is employed to try and stop him. He also has to act as mentor to a young Christian lieutenant, Garnett DeBuin (Bruce Davison), who is shocked by the gruesome acts perpetrated by Ulzana.

Comments: Generally the film avoids depicting violence on screen, though it is famous for one scene in which some Indians tear out a man's heart and toss it to each other. Terrorism is portrayed as reducing both terrorist and pursuer to the level of crude violence.

The Frisco Kid (1979)

Written by: Michael Elias and Frank Shaw

Plot: An orthodox Polish rabbi, Avram Belinski (Gene Wilder) is sent off to lead a Jewish community in San Francisco. After having his money stolen in Philadelphia he continues his journey on foot. He finally joins an outlaw with a heart of gold, Tommy Lillard (Harrison Ford), and they endure many misadventures and calamities together.

Comments: A light frothy piece of fun, poking fun at both the western and Judaism. There is also a decent amount of action peppered throughout the comedy.

BUDD BOETTICHER

b.1916. d. 2001.

After studying at Ohio State University Boetticher went to Mexico and trained to become an expert matador. It was through his friendship with Hal Roach Jr., director and producer and son of Hal Roach Sr., creator of the Laurel and Hardy films, that he managed to gain a foothold in the film industry. One of his earliest jobs was as technical adviser on a film about bullfighting called *Blood and Sand* (1941), directed by Rouben Mamoulian. His first film of note as a director was produced by John

Wayne and was a fictionalised account of his own experiences in Mexico, called *The Bullfighter and the Lady* (1951). The film was re-edited by John Ford, who Boetticher regarded as his mentor, with Boetticher's agreement. The sequence of westerns which made him famous came from a partnership with the actor Randolph Scott and the team of Harry Joe Brown as producer and Burt Kennedy as writer. He also helped Audie Murphy start his career in westerns at this time. In 1958 he directed some of the popular TV series *77 Sunset Strip*. In 1960 he also made a gangster film which became well known: *The Rise and Fall of Legs Diamond*. He then spent seven years in Mexico making a documentary about a famous matador named Carlos Arruza, but endured much suffering in the process, including serious illness, divorce, imprisonment and incarceration in a mental institution. The film *Arruza* appeared in 1972. On his return to Hollywood he made one more feature with the actor Audie Murphy. He completed another documentary film and was planning further features. He died at the age of 85.

The Wolf Hunters (1949)

B&W.
Written by: Scott Darling

Plot: Four fur trappers are killed and their furs stolen. Corporal Rod Webb (Kirby Grant) of the Royal Northwest Mounted Police has the task of investigating the deaths. On the way he finds another trapper, who has been shot and is lying unconscious. Webb attempts to track the man who tried to kill him with the aid of his dog Chinook. He is helped in his search by an Indian servant, Minnetaki (Elizabeth Root), and also the wife of the superintendent of the trading company, Marcia Cameron (Helen Parrish).

Comments: Not a western that has caused much stir, but it was a good run-of-the-mill production and demonstrates Boetticher's confident direction.

The Cimarron Kid (1952)

Written by: Louis Stevens

Plot: A young man, Bill Doolin, known as The Cimarron Kid (Audie Murphy), who had some connection to the infamous Dalton gang, is falsely accused by corrupt railroad officials of helping in one of their robberies. He subsequently joins the gang and takes part in other robberies. He is eventually betrayed by another gang member and tries to escape in the company of that member's daughter to South America.

Comments: The first in a series Boetticher made with Audie Murphy. It's interesting for the inclusion of a black actor in a prominent role (Frank Silvera as Stacey), which was uncommon at this time. He shares equally in the proceeds of the gang's crimes and is also shown in a scene at home with his family, revealing his preference for a life away from crime.

Bronco Buster (1952)

Written by: Horace McCoy

Plot: The story of two friends, Tom Moody (John Lund) helps Bart Eaton (Scott Brady) learn how to become a good rodeo performer. Eaton becomes successful and rich, and arrogant about his prowess, before finally learning some humility.

Comments: The film is most notable for its realistic depiction of the lives of rodeo stars. The stunts actually took place and no faked shots were included. Boetticher used his own knowledge as an experienced horseman and brought in expert rodeo men to perform and advise.

Horizons West (1952)

Written by: Louis Stevens

Plot: After the Civil War, Dan Hammond (Robert Ryan) and his brother Neil (Rock Hudson) return to their home in Texas. Their lives develop in different ways. Dan becomes a cattle rustler, and Neil a marshal. Dan kills his rival Cord Hardin (Raymond Burr) and courts his widow Lorna (Julie Adams). His lifestyle leads to an inevitable confrontation between the two brothers.

Comments: The film is archetypal with its confrontation of two brothers. It is also full of classic images of the West, with brilliant skies and sweeping landscapes in glorious Technicolor.

Seminole (1953)

Written by: Charles K Peck

Plot: The story is set at Fort King in 1835 in what was then known as the Florida Territory. Lieutenant Lance Caldwell (Rock Hudson) is being court-martialed on the charge of killing a sentry after an uneasy peace between the settlers and the Indians was threatened by the anti-Indian behaviour of the commander of the fort, Major Harlan Degan (Richard Carlson). It is he who accuses Caldwell of killing a soldier while he was trying to restore peace.

Comments A well-constructed and well-executed story. Boetticher was one of the first directors to treat the Indian characters with respect and allow them a dignified status in his films.

The Man from the Alamo (1953)

Written by: DD Beauchamp and Steve Fisher

Plot: John Stroud (Glenn Ford) is chosen by lot during the siege of the Alamo to escape and warn the others' families of the impending danger. After he escapes he is regarded as a coward by most people. Then the families are killed by renegades and Stroud seeks out those responsible.

Comments: Good action sequences are combined with great sensitivity of characterisation and well-wrought dialogue in this original perspective on the classic Alamo story.

Wings of the Hawk (1953)

Written by: Kay Lenard and James E Moser

Plot: 'Irish' Gallagher (Van Heflin) is an American engineer whose gold mine is confiscated by Colonel Ruiz (George Dolenz) of the Mexican provisional government, and he finds himself caught up in the Mexican Revolution (1910–11). He saves the life of the leader of the rebels, Raquel Noriega (Julie Adams), and develops a relationship with her. He finally finds himself obliged to destroy his own mine.

Comments: The film combines good pace with convincing characterisation. It is interesting to note that it was originally released in the 3-D process. The title refers to the falcon emblem on the Mexican flag.

Seven Men From Now (1956)

Written by: Burt Kennedy

Plot: Ben Stride (Randolph Scott) is a former lawman whose wife has been killed in a robbery. He feels partly responsible for her death due to the fact that his inability to keep his job made it necessary for his wife to work in the Wells Fargo express office where the robbery took place. He hunts down the seven men who are responsible for killing her.

Comments: The film is generally considered to be one of Boetticher's most accomplished westerns, combining stylish cinematography and a tightly wrought plot, and featuring excellent performances from all the principals. After its first showing it remained forgotten for about 40 years, retained in the vaults of Batjac Productions. It is interesting to note that John Wayne was responsible for getting Boetticher to look at the screenplay. Wayne and the accomplished director Andrew McLaglen (see several films included in chapter 7) were both producers for the film, together with Robert E Morrison. It is one of Boetticher's own favourites.

The Tall T (1957)

Written by: Burt Kennedy

Plot: Pat Brennan (Randolph Scott) is returning to his ranch on a stage-coach which belongs to a honeymoon couple, Willard (John Hubbard) and Doretta (Maureen O'Sullivan) Mims. When Brennan gets off the coach at a way station, it is taken over by three outlaws, Frank Usher (Richard Boone), Billy Jack (Skip Homeier) and Chink (Henry Silva). Willard Mims proves to be a coward, concerned only to save his own skin. He does a deal by which the outlaws will write a ransom note to Mrs Mims' wealthy father and let him go free.

Comments: The strength of the film lies in the carefully developed relationship between Pat and Usher, and in Boetticher's subtle direction and imaginative use of camera movement, blending psychological insight with convincing action.

Decision at Sundown (1957)

Written by: Charles Lang Jr.

Plot: Bart Allison (Randolph Scott) rides into the town of Sundown looking for the man, Tate Kimbrough (John Carroll), who he believes killed his wife. He finds Kimbrough and threatens him but gets trapped together with his friend Sam (Noah Beery Jr.) by the sheriff and his men who are in the pay of Kimbrough. When Sam is shot in the back many of the townsfolk turn against their sheriff and disarm his deputies.

Comments: The strength of Randolph Scott's performance here is the way in which he convincingly demonstrates the non-heroic aspects of his character, especially his human weaknesses: at one point he openly admits his fear. Throughout the film Boetticher shows clear preference for the subtle use of understatement.

Buchanan Rides Alone (1958)

Written by: Burt Kennedy and Charles Lang Jr.

Plot: Tom Buchanan (Randolph Scott) rides into the town of Agry in West Texas, named after the Agry family, and finds himself in the midst of a feud between several members of the family. When Buchanan tries to help a Mexican who seeks revenge on one member of the family he finds that he is taking on the whole clan.

Comments: This is another accomplished film in the series Boetticher made with Randolph Scott and the excellent scriptwriter Burt Kennedy. It shares with the others a simple, clear style, and psychological insights are indicated with great subtlety. Understatement is the order of the day, not only in the dialogue but also in the central performances.

Westbound (1959)

Written by: Berne Giler

Plot: Captain John Hayes (Randolph Scott) establishes a stagecoach line during the Civil War to transport gold from Colorado to the Federal Treasury in the North, but he meets the opposition of a rich rancher, whose daughter was once Hayes' girlfriend. He also has to deal with Confederate attempts to relieve him of the gold.

Comments: Hardly the best of the seven westerns that Boetticher made with Randolph Scott, perhaps because he didn't use his favourite screenplay writer, Burt Kennedy. He also made it with a different production company, Warner Bros. rather than Columbia.

Ride Lonesome (1959)

Written by: Burt Kennedy

Plot: Ben Brigade (Randolph Scott) is a bounty hunter, once a sheriff, who is intent on getting the reward for a young murderer, Billy John (James Best), by taking him to Santa Cruz. When he stops at a trading post he saves the manager's wife (Karen Steele) from an attack by Indians. Here he also enlists the help of two outlaws, Sam Boone (Pernell Roberts) and Whit (James Coburn). Billy John's brother, Frank (Lee Van Cleef), wants to rescue his brother and is following Brigade with his gang.

Comments: There is much terse, witty dialogue in the film, set for the most part amidst a roughly beautiful landscape. It maintains a constant tension and compelling pace throughout The film also marks the screen debut of James Coburn.

Comanche Station (1960)

Written by: Burt Kennedy

Plot: Jefferson Cody (Randolph Scott) goes into Comanche territory to try to bring back a woman, Nancy Lowe (Nancy Gates), held prisoner by the Indians. He is also motivated by the fact that his own wife had been captured by Indians many years before. He is unaware that the woman's husband has advertised a reward of $5,000 for her return, dead or alive, and a gang of outlaws are determined to get the money.

Comments: Up to the usual high standards of Boetticher films, with well-written dialogue by Burt Kennedy and excellent location shooting by Charles Lawton Jr.

A Time for Dying (1969)

Written by: Budd Boetticher

Plot: Cass Dunning (Richard Lapp), a would-be gunfighter, saves a girl, Nellie (Anne Randall), from a life of prostitution but is forced to marry her by Judge Roy Bean (Victor Jory). Then the couple meet Jesse James (Audie Murphy) and his brother Frank, famed for being fast on the draw, who advises Cass that his shooting skills are not yet up to scratch.

Comments: This was Boetticher's last western and Audie Murphy's last film; he died in a light airplane crash in 1971 and the film was released after his death. Boetticher wrote his own screenplay, and while the film displays many of the stylistic characteristics of his earlier westerns, it is not quite so accomplished as the series made with Randolph Scott. It was also made after Boetticher's return to the USA from Mexico where he made the documentary about the matador Carlos Arruza.

MICHAEL CURTIZ

b. 1886. d. 1962.

Curtiz was born in Hungary in 1886, where he also started acting in and directing films. He studied and worked in Denmark for a while, and after World War One he continued making films in Hungary, Austria and Germany He moved to the USA in 1926, and started making films for Warner Bros. Amongst other classics in various genres he directed *Angels with Dirty Faces* (1938), *Casablanca* (1942), *Yankee Doodle Dandy* (1942), *Mildred Pierce* (1945) and *White Christmas* (1954). It is generally considered that the films he made when he left Warner Bros. in the 1950s did not match his earlier ones for quality.

Under a Texas Moon (1930)

Written by: Gordon Rigby

Plot: Don Carlos (Frank Fay) and two companions arrive in a small town called Fiesta, where they not only enjoy chatting up the pretty local girls but also decide to try and win the reward for capturing some outlaws who are rustling cattle.

Comments: This film is reputed to be the first sound western which was also in colour. Only one original print is said to have survived, though it has been faithfully copied. It was shot in early Technicolor and Curtiz made a point of displaying sequences with as many rich colours as possible. Critics have noted that the film reveals several typical Curtiz touches in the direction, including an impressive tracking shot in the final sequence. Also surprising for the period is a nude swimming sequence. The appearance of a young Myrna Loy in the role of Lolita Romero is interesting for fans of the star system.

River's End (1930)

B&W.
Written by: Charles Kenyon

Plot: Sergeant Conniston, of the Royal Canadian Mounted Police (played by Charles Bickford), searches for an escaped murderer named John Keith with the help of an alcoholic guide, Pat O'Toole (J Farrell MacDonald). When they finally catch up with Keith it turns out that he is Conniston's double (and also played by Charles Bickford). Conniston dies in the snow from the severe cold, and O'Toole becomes convinced that Keith is innocent of the murder and helps him disguise himself as Conniston. The woman whom Conniston had unsuccessfully pursued, Miriam (Evalyn Knapp), becomes intrigued by the changed personality of 'Conniston', and emotional complications ensue.

Comments: There is unfortunately little to recommend this film with its unlikely convoluted plot (which one might sum up as 'Mountie gets Man. Man gets Mountie. Man, as Mountie, gets Girl.') but the leading actors turn in decent performances.

Gold Is Where You Find It (1938)

Written by: Robert Buckner and Warren Duff

Plot: A feud develops over the discovery of gold in California between the farmers who own the land and miners seeking the gold. Tensions are exacerbated when the daughter (Olivia de Havilland) of a wheat farmer becomes emotionally involved with an employee (George Brent) of a mining company.

Comments: While the film has been praised for its production values, and its use of a quasi-documentary narration at the beginning and end, it tells a rather conventional and predictable story.

Dodge City (1939)

Written by: Robert Buckner

Plot: An Irish soldier of fortune, Wade Hutton (Errol Flynn), arrives in Dodge City to find the city a den of corruption and lawlessness, mainly under the control of the gambling saloon owner, Jeff Surrett (Bruce Cabot). Hutton takes over the role of sheriff, captures the hearts of both a saloon girl (Ann Sheridan) and the more morally upright Abbie Irving (Olivia de Havilland), and finally cleans out the corrupt elements in the city.

Comments: The film has been greatly praised for its energetic pace and especially for the brilliantly choreographed barroom brawl, which has been imitated and indeed pirated in many films and TV productions since. The film was Errol Flynn's first western and his character was made Irish to explain away his inconvenient Australian accent. He made eight westerns altogether for Warner Bros.

Virginia City (1940)

B&W.
Written by: Robert Buckner

Plot: Set during the Civil War, a Union officer, Captain Kerry Bradford (Errol Flynn), escapes from a Confederate prison camp, and, arriving in Virginia City, Nevada, finds out that the former commander of the same prison camp, Captain Vance Irby (Randolph Scott), is planning to send gold to the value of $5 million to support a final attempt by the Confederates to stage a successful uprising. Bradford decides to thwart his plans.

Comments: The film is full of action, though little care was paid to historical accuracy. It is notable for the lively performances of Alan Hale and Guinn 'Big Boy' Williams as Bradford's eccentric companions and for the amusing miscasting of Humphrey Bogart as a Mexican outlaw with a poor Spanish accent and very unconvincing moustache. The musical score is very enjoyable for its incorporation of several traditional songs, such as 'The Battle Hymn of the Republic' and 'Oh Susannah'.

Santa Fe Trail (1940)

B&W.
Written by: Robert Buckner

Plot: Two West Point graduates of 1854 agree not to let their political differences disturb their friendship. Jeb Stuart (Errol Flynn) is from the South and George Armstrong Custer (Ronald Reagan) is from the North. They do, however, find themselves competing for the affections of Kit Carson Holliday (Olivia de Havilland). The two officers go to serve at Fort Leavenworth, Kansas, where the westward Santa Fe Trail starts. They are given the task of capturing, dead or alive, John Brown (Raymond Massey), the fanatical campaigner for the abolition of slavery. The climax involves Brown's seizure of the arsenal at Harpers Ferry, his capture and eventual execution.

Comments: The film has been severely criticised for its historical inaccuracy and biased account of John Brown's beliefs. The main officers featured, who were historical personages, did not all graduate from West Point in 1854, and the Harpers Ferry incident is not adequately explained. The accusation that the film presents John Brown as little more than a religious fanatic is unfair, for, while he was certainly fanatical, his views on the slavery issue are referred to in the film on several occasions as basically sound. Special praise has been given to Van Heflin for his performance as a former West Point cadet who decides to support Brown.

The Boy from Oklahoma (1954)

Written by: Frank Davis and Winston Miller

Plot: Tom Brewster (Will Rogers Jr.), who wants to become a lawyer, is a deft hand at using a lasso but not a gun. He is nevertheless offered a job as sheriff. He at first refuses, but eventually agrees. Despite the absence of a gun he pursues the murderer of the former sheriff, who turns out to be the very man who proposed him for the job. Love interest is provided through Brewster's wooing of the pretty Katie Brannigan (Nancy Olson).

Comments: It is a pleasant enough lightweight film, which also spawned a TV series that became popular in the USA. The TV series was called *Sugarfoot* and had many of the same characters and actors as the film.

The Proud Rebel (1958)

Written by: Lillie Hayward and Joseph Petracca

Plot: An ex-Confederate soldier, John Chandler (Alan Ladd), is seeking medical help for his son (played by Ladd's own son David) who became mute through the trauma of seeing his mother killed and their home destroyed by fire when the Union army attacked Atlanta. In a small town in Illinois, Chandler is arrested for getting in a fight with the two sons of a sheep farmer, Harry Burleigh (Dean Jagger). He is helped by a woman, Linnett Moore (Olivia de Havilland), who owns a farm which Burleigh would like to take over. Chandler repays the woman's help by working for her. She becomes fond of both father and son.

Comments: A moving film, in which the relationships are explored subtly and well. With its child and dog interest, some consider it too much of a family film. David Ladd, who was 11 years old at the time, became famous through its release.

The Hangman (1959)

B&W.
Written by: Dudley Nichols

Plot: A deputy marshal, Mackenzie Bovard (Robert Taylor), known as 'The Hangman' for his ability to track down murderers, is searching for Johnny Bishop (Jack Lord), who was involved in a hold up. He attempts to enlist the man's former girlfriend (played by Tina Louise) by offering her money if she will come with him to identify Bishop. Eventually it is discovered that Bishop is now living a normal life as a respected member of a community, helping other men to relinquish lives of crime. The local people are reluctant to hand him over to the law.

Comments: Lacking many of the characteristics of the average western – there are, for example, few outdoor scenes – it is well written and well performed, and explores complex moral issues. A sense of humanity prevails over the letter of the law.

The Comancheros (1961)

Written by: James Edward Grant and Clair Huffaker

Plot: A Texas Ranger, Jake Cutter (John Wayne), arrests a gambler, Paul Regret (Stuart Whitman), on a shooting charge. Regret helps him in a surprise attack by Indians, and the Rangers invite Regret to join them. Cutter and Regret are given the job of rounding up some outlaws, known as the 'Comancheros', who are running guns and alcohol to the Indians.

Comments: The film has been justly praised for its tense, witty dialogue, and for dealing with moral issues with a deft, light touch. Various historical inaccuracies have been identified in the film – for example the date when firearms were introduced – but they are essentially minor details and don't invalidate the central issues. A comic cameo by the actor Guinn 'Big Boy' Williams, appearing as a gun runner who is so stupid that he does not realise why he is being arrested, is memorable not only in its own right but as the last performance by the veteran actor, who died shortly after making the film. It was also Michael Curtiz' last film. He was so ill with cancer during the making of it that John Wayne had to take over much of the directing, though he refused to be credited for it. The landscapes in Arizona and Utah are stunningly shot in Cinemascope, and there is a stirring musical score by Elmer Bernstein.

DELMER DAVES

b. 1904. d. 1977.

Daves' parents came from pioneer stock, and his grandfather had been a pony express rider. When Daves was young he spent a lot of time on the reservations of the Navajo and Hopi Indians and retained an interest in their lives and history. He studied law at Stanford University but while still at college he got a job as a prop boy for *The Covered Wagon* (1923). He went on to work as technical advisor on several films before working as an actor, writing screenplays and his own stories. He wrote scripts for some successful films in Hollywood in the 1930s and 1940s. His first success as a director was *Destination Tokyo* in 1943.

Broken Arrow (1950)

Written by: Albert Maltz and Michael Blankfort

Plot: A veteran of the Civil War, Tom Jeffords (James Stewart) is an army scout who is concerned about the way Indians are treated and tries to establish peace between the settlers and the Apache Indians. He also becomes involved in a love affair with a beautiful Indian girl called Sonseeahray (Debra Paget).

Comments: The film received the Golden Globe Award for Best Film

Promoting International Understanding for its sympathetic and respectful treatment of the American Indians. A notable feature of the film is Jeff Chandler's sensitive and intelligent portrayal of the Apache chief Cochise. The film has a tragic ending, however, and the mixed race relationship is not allowed to be consummated. Neither audiences nor studios in the America of the 1950s were ready yet for a more liberal outcome.

Return of the Texan (1952)

B&W.
Written by: Dudley Nichols

Plot: A widower, Sam Crockett (Dale Robertson), returns to his farm in Texas with his two sons and his father (Walter Brennan) to try and set up a new life. He gets a job working for a neighbour, Rod (Richard Boone), whose sister-in-law, Ann Marshall (Joanne Dru), falls in love with him, but he cannot forget his wife.

Comments: The film frequently verges on the tragic but manages to avoid it. It reveals a love of and respect for nature throughout, especially through the character of the grandfather.

Drum Beat (1954)

Written by: Delmer Daves

Plot: A frontiersman, Johnny MacKay (Alan Ladd), negotiates a peace treaty on behalf of President Ulysses S Grant with the Modoc Indians in Northern California. He feels strong resentment against Indians in general, as they slaughtered his family some years before, but tries to accomplish his task without the use of force. The leader of the Modoc, however, known as 'Captain Jack' (Charles Bronson), is warlike and strongly antipathetic to the government.

Comments: Featuring two superlative performances by Alan Ladd and Charles Bronson, the film did much to help Bronson establish himself as a leading actor, capable of more than minor roles.

Jubal (1956)

Written by: Delmer Daves and Russell S Hughes

Plot: Jubal Troop (Glenn Ford) is offered a job by a rancher, Shep Horgan (Ernest Borgnine). When Shep makes Jubal his foreman, this makes another hand, Pinky (Rod Steiger), jealous and angry. He had previously been the lover of Shep's wife Mae (Valerie French). Pinky tells Shep that Jubal has been having an affair with Mai. When emotions become heated a killing ensues.

Comments: Based on the novel *Jubal Troop* by Paul Wellman, the film never lets up on suspense and includes powerful performances from all the main actors. Particularly moving is Ernest Borgnine as the well-intentioned but passionate husband; comparisons can be drawn with the story of Othello.

The Last Wagon (1956)

Written by: Delmer Daves and James Edward Grant

Plot: Comanche Todd (Richard Widmark) has been convicted of murdering three brothers in revenge for their murder of his Indian wife. He is being transported in chains by wagon train. When there is an attack by Apache Indians he is given the task of taking six surviving children to safety. Eventually he is brought to account for his past crimes.

Comments: This film has not received the attention it deserves. It features a powerful and convincing performance by Richard Widmark, and reflects Daves' lifelong concern about the treatment of Indians by the white settlers.

3.10 to Yuma (1957)

B&W.
Written by: Halsted Welles

Plot: Dan Evans (Van Heflin) has problems paying debts for his ranch and agrees to take on the job of accompanying the captured outlaw Ben Wade (Glenn Ford) on the 3.10 train to Yuma. Wade's gang are planning to set him free, but no one in the town is willing to support Evans, except the town drunk played by Henry Jones. So he has to wait alone for the inevitable confrontation, as time ticks away before the arrival of the train, with Wade constantly seeking to undermine his self-confidence.

Comments: The film clearly derives one of its main methods of creating suspense (the ticking away of time until a crucial moment) from Zinnemann's *High Noon* (1952). It is a powerful drama in its own right, however, with strong, notable performances in the central roles from Heflin and Ford.

Cowboy (1958)

Written by: Dalton Trumbo and Edmund H North

Plot: Frank Harris (Jack Lemmon) works as a clerk at a hotel in Chicago. When he meets a cattleman called Tom Reese (Glenn Ford), he persuades him to take him on his next cattle drive, from Chicago to the Rio Grande. At first he is easily shocked and disturbed by many experiences on the way, but eventually becomes hardened to the ways of cowboys. Each man gradually learns to respect the other.

Comments: Yes, this film is about *the* Frank Harris who wrote the notorious memoirs of his sexual exploits *My Life and Loves* (1922). He also wrote his reminiscences of life as a cowboy which were first incorporated in a later edition of the famous book, and later published separately under the title *On the Trail*. Which sequences in both book and film are actually based on fact is open for debate, but it has made for an enjoyable, good-humoured film, with both the leading actors providing believable performances, though Lemmon's Frank Harris is far removed from his historical counterpart. The character had already been 'cleaned up' in the course of scriptwriting.

The Badlanders (1958)

Written by: Richard Collins

Plot: Peter van Hoek (Alan Ladd), known as 'The Dutchman', is released from prison in Arizona along with John McBain (Ernest Borgnine). Van Hoek wants to take revenge on the inhabitants of a small mining town who are responsible for unjustly imprisoning him. McBain is determined to leave criminal ways behind him, but is drawn into a plan of van Hoek's to carry out a gold robbery.

Comments: Based on the novel 'The Asphalt Jungle' by WR Burnett, the two central characters are nicely contrasted in terms of character and moral values, and the film has moments of comedy to relieve the suspense.

The Hanging Tree (1959)

Written by: Wendell Mayes and Halsted Welles

Plot: A doctor, Joe Frail (Gary Cooper), is trying to escape from memories of a personal tragedy and arrives in a gold-mining town in Montana. He saves a man (Ben Piazza) who is accused of being a thief from a posse of lawmen, and they become good friends. He also nurses back to health a Swiss woman, Elizabeth Mahler (Maria Schell). However, when Frenchy (Karl Malden) tries to rape Elizabeth, Joe shoots him and throws his body over a cliff. He is caught by the townspeople who decide to hang him. Only Elizabeth is determined to save him.

Comments: A perceptive study of psychological change. The film concentrates more on the relationships than on action. It also featured the first film performance by George C Scott, as Dr. George Grubb, a quack religious healer.

CLINT EASTWOOD

b.1930

Born in San Francisco, the son of a steelworker, Eastwood managed to get his first small roles in B-rated films, achieving his first popular success with the TV western series *Rawhide*, which started in 1959. He made his breakthrough as an actor with three of the so-called 'spaghetti westerns' directed by Sergio Leone: *A Fistful of Dollars* (1964), *For a Few Dollars More* (1965), and *The Good, The Bad, and The Ugly* (1966). Eastwood went on to appear in such popular blockbusters as *Where Eagles Dare* (1968), *Coogan's Bluff* (1968), and *Kelly's Heroes* (1970). He also starred in the extremely successful thriller *Dirty Harry* (1971). In the same year he made his debut as director with *The Beguiled* and *Play Misty For Me*, in which he also starred. The first western he directed was *High Plains Drifter* (1973), in which he also starred as the nameless stranger. In 1976 the western *The Outlaw Josey Wales* appeared, which he directed and also acted in. *Bronco Billy* (1980) could be classed as a western, due to its central setting of a Wild West Show, but is set in modern times. The next western which he directed and acted in was *Pale Rider* (1985), and his most accomplished western to date, as director and actor, is undoubtedly *Unforgiven* (1992), which is discussed also in Chapter 11.

High Plains Drifter (1973)

Written by: Ernest Tidyman

Plot: A mysterious stranger (Clint Eastwood) arrives in the town of Lago.

He is goaded into a gunfight by three men, whom he kills without compunction. He is then hired by the townsfolk to protect them from some outlaws who have just been released from prison. The outlaws had brutally whipped the former sheriff of the town to death when he threatened to disclose that the town's wealth was based on illegal mining. The townsfolk let the three take the blame for the murder and now they are afraid that the men will want revenge.

Comments: The film was undoubtedly influenced by Eastwood's experience of working with Sergio Leone, and there is a shot in the film of a gravestone inscribed with Leone's name, in joking homage. The central mysterious character, the bleak setting, and the stark brutality of the action, are all reminiscent of the 'spaghetti western'. The stranger is clearly not a moral force but seeks revenge with cold calculation. He is also far from the mould of the conventional western hero: when a young woman provokes him he rapes her.

The Outlaw Josey Wales (1976)

Written by: Sonia Chernus and Phil Kaufman

Plot: At the time of the Civil War a Missouri farmer, Josey Wales (Clint Eastwood), discovers that his family has been murdered by Union soldiers and he decides to fight for the Confederates. The Confederate soldiers are persuaded to surrender to the Union soldiers, but the Union commander, Terrill (Bill McKinney), executes most of the Confederates. Wales discovers that this commander was also responsible for the murder of his family. He escapes, helps an Indian friend and a family of farmers, and eventually he sets up a small community on the land owned by two white women he has helped, convincing the Indians that they can live and work together.

Comments: There are extensive scenes of violence in the film, but the final message of the film is not that human nature is essentially violent but that coexistence and harmony between races is possible. There is consistently impressive cinematography by Bruce Surtees throughout the film, especially in its dramatic use of the contrast of light and shade.

Pale Rider (1985)

Written by: Michael Butler and Dennis Schryack

Plot: Set in California in 1850, the film tells of some independent gold miners and their families who are terrorised by the head of a strip-mining corporation, Coy LaHood (Richard Dysart), who wants to obtain their land. Hull Barrett (Michael Moriarty) leads the protests against LaHood, trying to solve the problems peacefully, to protect his girlfriend, Sarah (Carrie Snodgress), and her young daughter, Megan (Sydney Penny). A mysterious stranger, known only as 'The Preacher' (Clint Eastwood) arrives, and helps the independent miners in their fight.

Comments: The similarities to the plot of George Stevens' *Shane* (1953) are undeniable, with the exception that the young boy in the earlier film is replaced by a girl. Eastwood's film is much darker, however, infused with a more pervasive sense of evil, and the viewer is given the disturbing feeling that there is a quasi-mystical force seeking vengeance through the agency of 'The Preacher'. This feeling is present from the very moment of the stranger's appearance, when the young girl sees him while she's reading about Death on a 'pale horse' in the Book of Revelation.

Unforgiven (1992)

Written by: David Webb Peoples

Plot: Some men are arrested for the mutilation of a prostitute (Anna Thomson) in the town of Big Whiskey, Wyoming, but the sheriff, Little Billy Daggett (Gene Hackman), lets them go. The other prostitutes in the town offer a reward for the capture of the cowboy responsible. William Munny (Clint Eastwood), who had once been an outlaw but turned to pig farming, decides to try and win the reward in order to support his two children after the death of their mother. He is aided by a former partner in crime, Ned Logan (Morgan Freeman), and the young Schofield Kid (Jaimz Woolvett). The climax is very violent and entails the deaths of several of the main protagonists. Munny survives to try and establish a new life for himself and his children far from Big Whiskey.

Comments: The film won great acclaim for Eastwood as a director and won four Academy Awards: for Best Picture, Best Director, Best Supporting Actor (Gene Hackman), and Best Editing (Joel Cox). It is a dark, disturbing film, as are the other westerns he directed. One of the people he dedicated the film to was Sergio Leone, whose 'spaghetti westerns' brought Eastwood his international fame as an actor. The influence of the Italian's bleak view of human nature is still evident, as are elements of his visual style, though the dialogue is richer and more earthy.

JOHN FORD

b. 1894. d. 1973.

Born John Martin Feeney in America to parents from County Galway, Ireland, Ford started his career as a stage actor under the name Jack Ford, and played a walk-on role in DW Griffith's *The Birth of a Nation* (1915). He eventually turned to directing and also served as president of the Motion Picture Directors Association during the 1920s. During World War Two he served in the navy and made documentaries for the Navy Department. After the war he became a rear admiral in the US Navy Reserve. He won four Academy Awards as Best Director for non-western films *The Informer* (1935), *The Grapes of Wrath* (1940), *How Green Was My Valley* (1941) and *The Quiet Man* (1952). Other notable films in his long career are *The Lost Patrol* (1934), *Young Mr Lincoln* (1939), *Tobacco Road* (1941), and *Donovan's Reef* (1963), amongst others. He acted in several westerns before directing his first, *The Tornado* (1917), and he made about 42 silent westerns in all before his first sound western, and a major landmark in the genre, *Stagecoach* (1939).

Stagecoach (1939)

B&W.
Written by: Dudley Nichols

Plot: The plot follows the various events that befall a group of passengers aboard a stagecoach travelling to Lordsburg. They find themselves caught between two frontier towns when Apache Indians are on the warpath. The group consists of nine very different individuals: a girl from a dance hall, Dallas (Claire Trevor); a sheriff, Curly (George Bancroft); the stagecoach driver, Buck (Andy Devine); a gambler, Hatfield (John Carradine); a corrupt banker, Gatewood (Berton Churchill); an alcoholic doctor, Doc Boone (Thomas Mitchell); a nervous seller of whisky, Peacock (Donald Meek); and an army officer's pregnant wife, Lucy Mallory (Louise Platt). They are joined by an escaped prisoner, the Ringo Kid (John Wayne), who is bent on taking revenge for the murder of his father and brother at the end of their journey.

Comments: The film was a landmark for several reasons. It was the first western by John Ford to lift his work clearly out of the 'B' western category, and it established John Wayne once and for all as a major star. All the elements which distinguish a John Ford western are there: characters that represent different levels of society, with those who are frequently despised having to prove they have a good side; lovable rogues and despicable capitalists; the blend of suspense and comedy; the classic landscapes, particularly that of Monument Valley; gunfights and Indian attacks. The black-and-white cinematography and the subtle lighting make it visually pleasing, and sound effects are subtly employed to enhance the suspense. The musical score, by various composers, won one of several Oscars®, and consists of orchestrated versions of traditional American folk songs, a resource that Ford was to return to again and again. The film was based on a story by Ernest Haycox called 'Stage to Lordsburg', but added a few extra characters.

Drums Along the Mohawk (1939)

Written by: Lamar Trotti and Sonya Levien

Plot: Set in the period of the American Revolutionary War, the film follows a couple, Gil Martin (Henry Fonda) and wife Lana (Claudette Colbert), who try to set up home in the Mohawk Valley. They endure a series of catastrophes: their farm is burned down by Indians and their first child dies. Then Gil has to go off to fight. A second child is born, but the Indians attack again. While Gil is away all the local people are forced to move to a fort for their safety. Gil returns with reinforcements which save the day.

Comments: Due to its historical setting, before independence, it could be argued that the film is not strictly a western, yet several common ingredients are present: the plight of settlers, the threat of Indian attack and the role of the army as saviours. The film follows very faithfully the book by Walter D Edmonds on which it is based.

My Darling Clementine (1946)

B&W.
Written by: Samuel G Engel, Sam Hellman and Winston Miller

Plot: Wyatt Earp (Henry Fonda) and his brothers Virgil (Tim Holt), Morgan (Ward Bond) and James (Don Garner) are driving a herd of cattle and arrive on the outskirts of the town of Tombstone. Three of the brothers go into the town leaving James to guard the cattle. When they return the cattle have been stolen and their brother is dead. Wyatt takes on the job of marshal in Tombstone, befriends the consumptive Doc Holliday (Victor Mature), and with his help and his brothers' eventually confronts the gang led by Ike Clanton (Walter Brennan) who killed their brother, in a showdown at the OK Corral.

Comments: A very perceptive and subtle version of the famous events, with much attention paid to the detail of body language and careful psychological studies of character. Henry Fonda's Earp is undoubtedly a much more sensitive and morally aware man than his historical counterpart, and there are several liberties taken with historical facts, notably the death of Doc Holliday, which actually occurred six years later. The character of Clementine (Cathy Downs) is also an invention. It was one of the first westerns to garner international critical acclaim, winning the Silver Ribbon Award given by the Italian National Syndicate for Best Foreign Film in 1948.

Fort Apache (1948)

B&W.
Written by: Frank S Nugent

Plot: A former general in the Civil War, Owen Thursday (Henry Fonda) has been demoted to the rank of lieutenant colonel and sent to Fort Apache, an outpost in the desert. He sends Captain York (John Wayne) and Sergeant Beaufort (Pedro Armendáriz) to bring back the Apache chief Cochise who has taken his tribe into Mexico. Cochise is led to believe that he is just being invited to a meeting, but when he arrives he is confronted by Thursday and a large troop, and ordered back to his reservation. Captain York protests but to no avail. Cochise promptly attacks Thursday's forces, killing all except for York and his men. On returning to the fort, York covers up Thursday's ill-fated tactics and allows him to be perceived as a hero.

Comments: All the leading roles are well cast, and the relationships between the men convincingly realised, as are the lives of the frontier wives in their attempts to maintain some sort of home for husbands and children. The film has the usual Ford blend of male camaraderie, humorous interludes, romance and mounting suspense. It was the film debut of the actor John Agar (as Lieutenant O'Rourke), who was the husband of the leading lady, Shirley Temple. The film is generally considered to be the first of Ford's so-called 'cavalry trilogy', which included *Rio Grande* (1950) and *She Wore a Yellow Ribbon* (1949).

3 Godfathers (1948)

Written by: Laurence Stallings and Frank S Nugent

Plot: Three bandits discover a dying woman (Mildred Natwick) in the desert who gives birth to a child. They promise to take care of the child and struggle through the desert, two of them dying on the way, but one, Robert Marmaduke Hightower (John Wayne), succeeding in reaching civilisation with the child.

Comments: This was Ford's first colour feature film. Harry Carey Jr. turned in a particularly accomplished performance as one of the bandits, known as the 'Abilene Kid'. The story by Peter Kyne had already been made into a film several times: in 1916, directed by Edward Le Saint, and already by Ford himself in 1919 under the title *Marked Men*; by William Wellman entitled *Hell's Heroes* in 1929 (see under Wellman) and by Richard Boleslawski in 1936.

She Wore a Yellow Ribbon (1949)

Written by: Frank S Nugent and Laurence Stallings

Plot: A veteran officer, Captain Nathan Brittles (John Wayne), is about to retire but does not want to leave his post, where he has trained many of the men. He has one last mission, to try and prevent an Indian uprising, but also has to consider the situation of the women under his protection. There is love interest in the form of competition between two young lieutenants, Flint Cohill (John Agar) and Ross Penell (Harry Carey Jr.), for the love of Olivia Dandridge (Joanne Dru), for whom both want to wear a yellow ribbon in battle.

Comments: The film is the second in what is generally known as Ford's 'cavalry trilogy', with *Fort Apache* (1948) and *Rio Grande* (1950). John Wayne's performance is among the most sensitive of his career. He was playing a man more than a decade older than his real age. There are several memorable moments, such as when, for example, he fumbles for his glasses to read the inscription on the gold watch given him by his men, and his low-key monologue at his wife's grave. The rousing title song also haunts the memory long after viewing the film.

Wagon Master (1950)

B&W.
Written by: Patrick Ford and Frank S Nugent

Plot: Jonathan Wiggs (Ward Bond), the elder of a group of Mormons, hires two young horse traders, Travis Blue (Ben Johnson) and Sandy (Harry Carey Jr.), to lead a large group of Mormons to Utah. On the way they are joined by a family of outlaws called the Cleggs, hoping to use the wagon train as cover, and a troupe of rather dubious performers under Doc Hall (Alan Mowbray). They also encounter hostile Indians.

Comments: Not so well known as Ford's more popular westerns, this film has much to recommend it. There is a strong central performance by Ben Johnson in one of his few leading roles, and Ward Bond is compelling as the Mormon elder. The film also has a well-structured plot and many enjoyable cameo performances.

Rio Grande (1950)

B&W.
Written by: James Kevin McGuinness

Plot: During the Civil War, Lieutenant Colonel Kirby Yorke (John Wayne), a northerner, had to burn down the plantation of his estranged wife Kathleen (Maureen O'Hara), a southerner, on the orders of General Sheridan (J Carrol Naish); for 15 years Yorke sees neither wife nor son. He is frustrated at not being allowed to cross the border into Mexico in pursuit of marauding Indians. Then one day his son, Jeff, arrives as a new recruit, followed by Kathleen, who attempts to have their son removed from his post. The young man refuses to leave.

Comments: The third film in the so-called 'cavalry trilogy' by Ford, which includes *Fort Apache* (1948) and *She Wore a Yellow Ribbon* (1949), it includes several impressive action sequences, including one of Ben Johnson and Harry Carey Jr. doing their own stunts which involved them riding with one foot on each of two horses.

The Searchers (1956)

Written by: Frank S Nugent

Plot: An ex-Confederate soldier, Ethan Edwards (John Wayne), returns, about three years after the Civil War is over, to his brother's home in Texas. His brother, sister-in-law and nephew are killed in a Comanche attack and he sets out with his adopted nephew Martin (Jeffrey Hunter), who is half Indian, in search of his niece, Debbie, who is assumed to have survived and been taken by the Comanche chief Scar. For five years they travel, facing endless hardships and challenges, until finally they find the niece, who has now adopted Indian ways.

Comments: One of Ford's most moving and thought-provoking films, with a powerful performance by John Wayne at the height of his career. He created a complex and mysterious man, whose motivations are manifold and origins obscure. We never learn, for instance, what he was doing for those three years after the end of the Civil War. His hatred of Indians and his love of family almost tear him apart, emotions heightened by the presence of a half-Indian nephew and the discovery that his niece has been assimilated into an Indian way of life. As one would expect from Ford the film is not without its comic interludes, supplied by two characters which were an addition to the story on which the film was based ('The Avenging Texan' by Alan LeMay). Hank Worden plays a rather dim-witted old man called Mose Harper and Ward Bond is an odd priest, the Reverend Sam Clayton. As one expects with a Ford western, impressive landscapes form backdrops for, and inform, every stage of the drama. (See also chapter 6)

The Horse Soldiers (1959)

Written by: John Lee Mahin and Martin Rackin

Plot: During the Civil War the Union soldiers are having difficulty taking a high bluff over the Mississippi River. Colonel John Marlow (John Wayne) is sent to try to solve the impasse, by destroying a rail supply station with the aid of only three brigades of soldiers. There is constant disagreement between the authoritarian Marlow and the more liberal surgeon, Major Henry Kendall (William Holden). The situation is further complicated by the presence of Hannah Hunter (Constance Towers) who falls in love with Marlow.

Comments: Although not a successful film at the box office, the film has many strong points, not least the well-developed relationship between Marlow and Kendall. This was no doubt partially due to the fact that the two actors were friends in real life, and had a good working relationship with the director. The musical score incorporates many well-known Civil War songs. One memorable scene in the film takes place in a saloon when Marlow gets drunk and reveals why he hates doctors. It is the kind of set-piece performance which John Wayne handled with great panache.

Sergeant Rutledge (1960)

Written by: James Warner Bellah and Willis Goldbeck

Plot: Braxton Rutledge (Woody Strode) is a black cavalry sergeant in the Ninth Cavalry Regiment, an African-American army unit. He is accused of the rape and murder of a white woman and the ensuing murder of his commanding officer. His guilt appears to be confirmed when he deserts, but an old friend, Lieutenant Tom Cantrell (Jeffrey Hunter), is sent to bring him back, helping to put down an Apache uprising in the process, then agreeing to defend Braxton in court.

Comments: Based on a story by John and Ward Hawkins in 1955 called 'Shadow of the Noose', this was a landmark Hollywood film in the prominence it gave to a black actor. It is a compelling courtroom drama, though by modern standards does not probe the racial issues very deeply. By Ford's standards the film contains very few outdoor action scenes.

Two Rode Together (1961)

Written by: Frank S Nugent

Plot: A corrupt marshal, Guthrie McCabe (James Stewart), and a cavalry lieutenant, Jim Gary (Richard Widmark), join together to try and bring back people taken prisoner by the Comanche when they were children. When they finally reach the Comanche camp they find that the captives now no longer wish to return to their original families. They do manage to bring back two captives, including a young boy known by his Indian name of Running Wolf (David Kent), who murders the relative who claims him, and a Spanish woman, Elena de la Madriaga (Linda Cristal), who finds herself treated as an outcast because she was the lover of the Comanche chief Stone Calf (Woody Strode).

Comments: With its blend of seriousness and humour, this is characteristic Ford. It was not, however, a success at the box office, and nor was it well received by critics at the time. Ford also lost enthusiasm for the film when news reached him of the death of his longtime friend and stalwart actor Ward Bond.

The Man Who Shot Liberty Valance (1962)

B&W.
Written by: James Warner Bellah and Willis Goldbeck

Plot: A US senator Ransom Stoddard (James Stewart) returns with his wife Hallie (Vera Miles) to the town of Shinbone on the occasion of the funeral of their old friend, Tom Doniphon (John Wayne). The senator's life is not what it seems and he decides to tell his story to a young journalist. In the past the town had been terrorised by the vicious gunman Liberty Valance (Lee Marvin). Stoddard tried to get rid of Valance by legal means and the help of the local newspaper editor, Dutton Peabody (Edmond O'Brien). He came to realise, however, that the man could only be stopped by the use of violence, and he finally gunned down Valance – or so it seemed – becoming a local hero, and then elected to the senate. Eventually Doniphon revealed that it was he who actually shot Valance, but for the sake of Hallie, who had by then relinquished Doniphon and fallen in love with Stoddard, and in order to establish law and order in the town, Stoddard had to continue playing the hero.

Comments: At the end of the film, as the reporter starts to tear up his notes, Stoddard asks in surprise, 'You're not going to tell the story?' At this the reporter utters the oft-quoted lines, 'This is the West. When legend becomes fact, print the legend'. The film reveals the darker, less optimistic vision which characterised Ford's later films, and a figure, who was to feature in many later westerns, of the disenchanted man of the West, out of step with the times and the new moral values. Its style, employing many close-ups and more restricted settings, was unusual for Ford.

How the West Was Won (1962)

Note: This film was directed jointly with Henry Hathaway and George Marshall. For credits, plot and comments see entry under Henry Hathaway.

Cheyenne Autumn (1964)

Written by: James R Webb

Plot: The film tells the story of 300 or so Northern Cheyenne Indians trying to return from their present barren desert reserve in what is now Oklahoma to their ancestral homelands in the Dakotas, and how they are pursued over a 1,500-mile journey by the US Cavalry. They have been driven to this measure because the relevant government agency has failed to provide the supplies due to them according to the terms of a treaty. US Cavalry Captain Thomas Archer (Richard Widmark) has the job of bringing them back to their allotted territory, but he grows to respect their cause and decides to help them.

Comments: *Cheyenne Autumn* reveals much more sympathy for the plight of the Indians than any other film that Ford made, and events are viewed almost entirely from their perspective. Ford's last western, it is infused with a sad, disillusioned quality, autumnal indeed. The comic sequence set in Dodge City with James Stewart as Wyatt Earp bears no clear relation to the themes of the rest of the film, and functions almost as an intermission. Ford handed over the direction of part of the film to second unit director, Ray Kellogg. Despite its imperfections the film remains a moving and realistic depiction of the plight of such Indian tribes.

HENRY HATHAWAY

b. 1898 d. 1985.

The son of a theatre manager and a stage actress, Hathaway started acting in westerns as a child. After World War Two he briefly tried a career in business but then went to Hollywood to work under some famous directors, such as Josef von Sternberg and Victor Fleming. His first film as director was a western: *Heritage of the Desert* (1932). Especially well known are his films *The Desert Fox* (1951), about the Nazi field marshal Rommel, *Niagara* (1953), a thriller featuring Marilyn Monroe, *How the West Was Won* (1962), *Of Human Bondage* (1964), *True Grit* (1969), the western for which John Wayne finally got his Oscar®, and *Airport* (1970).

Heritage of the Desert (aka *When the West Was Young*) (1932)

B&W.
Written by: Frank Partos and Harold Shumate

Plot: A rancher, Adam Naab (J Farrell MacDonald), allows local ranchers to take their cattle through a narrow pass on his land, except one, Judd Holderness (David Landau), who is known to be a rustler. The situation is complicated by the arrival of a surveyor (Randolph Scott).

Comments: Despite its age the sound recording has worn well. There is some clever and effective editing in the film, which helps maintain suspense. The screenplay is based on a story by the famous writer of westerns Zane Grey. This was the first of a string of versions of Zane Grey stories that Hathaway made with Randolph Scott

Wild Horse Mesa (1932)

B&W.
Written by: Frank Howard Clark and Harold Shumate

Plot: A horse trainer (Randolph Scott) is concerned about the methods used to round up wild horses, which employ barbed wire and endanger the horses.

Comments: The story, by Zane Grey, was first made as a silent film in 1925, and made again as a sound film in 1947, directed by Wallace A Grissell and starring Tim Holt.

The Thundering Herd (1933)

B&W.
Written by: Jack Cunningham and Mary Flannery

Plot: Tom Doan (Randolph Scott) is a buffalo hunter who joins a wagon train heading west. Indians have been incited to fighting against the slaughter of their buffalo, and Doan tries to prevent them from attacking. There is also evidence of some dubious dealing in buffalo hides.

Comments: This version of the Zane Grey story is a remake of a silent film made in 1925, and some sequences of the earlier film are used in this version.

Under the Tonto Rim (1933)

B&W.
Written by: Jack Cunningham and Gerald Geraghty

Plot: A cowboy (Stuart Erwin) manages to capture a murderer with the help of the daughter of his boss.

Comments: The film was a remake of the silent film released in 1924, directed by Herman Raymaker, which was itself based on a story by Zane Grey.

Sunset Pass (1933)

B&W.
Written by: Jack Cunningham and Gerald Geraghty

Plot: A government agent (Randolph Scott) pretends to be a cowboy to find out who is rustling cattle, but he falls in love with the sister of the man who is suspected.

Comments: Another one of Hathaway's remakes of an earlier film (from 1929) and based on a story by Zane Grey. It was also one of seven films in which Hathaway directed Randolph Scott.

Man of the Forest (1933)

B&W.
Written by: Jack Cunningham and Harold Shumate

Plot: Brett Dale (Randolph Scott) tries to stop Clint Beasley (Noah Beery) from robbing Jim Gaynor (Harry Carey), an ex-convict, of his land and kidnapping the man's niece, Alice (Verna Hillie). The ex-convict tries to get his niece back but Beasley kills him and frames Dale for the murder.

Comments: Another of Hathaway's remakes of earlier Zane Grey westerns. This one features especially impressive cinematography by Ben F Reynolds.

To the Last Man (1933)

B&W.
Written by: Jack Cunningham

Plot: The film tells the story of a family feud in the period after the Civil War.

Comments: Not only one of the more interesting and well made of Hathaway's adaptations of Zane Grey stories, but also of historical interest for its unique casting. It includes not only Randolph Scott and Esther Ralston in the lead roles, but also Shirley Temple and John Carradine.

The Last Round-Up (1934)

B&W.
Written by: Jack Cunningham

Plot: A good-hearted outlaw, Jack Kells (Monte Blue), sacrifices his life for the sake of two lovers, Jim Cleve (Randolph Scott) and Joan Randall (Barbara Fritchie).

Comments: The film is an adaptation of Zane Grey's novel 'Border Region'.

Brigham Young (1940)

B&W.
Written by: Louis Bromfield and Lamar Trotti

Plot: The story follows the lot of a group of Mormons as they make their westward journey to what they believe is their promised land at Salt Lake in Utah. After the murder of their founder, Joseph Smith (Vincent Price), in prison, he becomes a martyr in the eyes of the movement, sparking the exodus led by Brigham Young (Dean Jagger) and his wife Mary Ann (Mary Astor). The story focuses on the relationship of two of the group, Jonathan Kent (Tyrone Power) and Zina Webb (Linda Darnell).

Comments: More than just a study of the Mormon movement and far from historically accurate, it nevertheless provides a fascinating study of the problems of religious doubt and the power of visionary belief.

Rawhide (1951)

B&W.
Written by: Dudley Nichols

Plot: Sam Todd (Edgar Buchanan), the manager of a stagecoach station, hears that a band of outlaws is in the neighbourhood and advises Vinnie Holt (Susan Hayward) and her young niece not to continue their journey but wait for the next coach. The outlaws arrive at the station and the manager is killed. His assistant, Tom Owens (Tyrone Power), is mistaken for the woman's husband and both are locked up. The outlaws await the arrival of a gold shipment, and the couple try to escape to warn the next coach.

Comments: Tension is well created during the build up to the arrival of the next stagecoach, and the sense of danger heightened by the presence of the vulnerable young child.

Garden of Evil (1954)

Written by: Frank Fenton

Plot: Leah Fuller (Susan Hayward) hires three men – a former sheriff, Hooker (Gary Cooper), a killer, Luke Daly (Cameron Mitchell), and a deceitful gambler, Fiske (Richard Widmark) – to rescue her husband who is trapped in a collapsed gold mine in an area known as the 'Garden of Evil'.

Comments: The film features many attractive broad landscape views and a charming village. It is an early example of the use of the Cinemascope process and Hathaway clearly wanted to make the most of it.

From Hell to Texas (1958)

Written by: Robert Buckner and Wencell Mayes

Plot: A cowboy, Tod Lohman (Don Murray), accidentally kills one of the sons of a rancher, Hunter Boyd (RG Armstrong). He is also blamed for the death of the second son in a stampede of horses. The rancher is determined to avenge the deaths of his sons, but Lohman saves the life of his third son, Tom (Dennis Hopper), who is trapped in a big fire.

Comments: The climax, which combines gunfight and a raging firestorm, is a breathtaking accomplishment, both exciting and harrowing to watch.

North to Alaska (1960)

Written by: John Lee Mahin, Martin Rackin and Claude Binyon

Plot: Two friends, Sam McCord (John Wayne) and George Pratt (Stewart Granger), find gold in Alaska. George sends Sam back to Seattle to fetch his fiancée, while he builds a home for them both. Sam finds that the so-called fiancée is already married. He decides to take a girl he met in a bar, Michelle (Capucine), back with him for George. Frankie Canon (Ernie Kovacs), who has been trying to steal the gold claim away from the two friends, turns out to be a former lover of Michelle's, and his passion reawakens.

Comments: A rollicking light-hearted film, with more than a touch of male chauvinism scattered throughout, it proved to be very successful at the box office on its first release.

How the West Was Won (1962)

Co-directors: John Ford and George Marshall
Written by: James R Webb

Plot: The film follows the lives of a family who set out from New England to settle in the West, over a period of 60 years, from 1839 to 1899. It encompasses all the major themes associated with the western genre: pioneers, the Civil War, Indian wars, buffalo stampedes, building railways, outlaws, law and order, and so on.

Comments: The direction of the film was shared between three directors. John Ford's section focused on the Civil War period; George Marshall handled the building of the railway and the stampeding buffalo; and Henry Hathaway's contribution encompassed the sequences about outlaws and the chases over the plains. The film has a remarkable array of Hollywood stars, including Henry Fonda, Gregory Peck, John Wayne, Karl Malden, Debbie Reynolds, James Stewart, and Richard Widmark, to name only a few, with Spencer Tracy as narrator. While the film is very ambitious in its scope, or perhaps because of this, its treatment of events is very superficial. It provides a dazzling spectacle, but only in a few sequences manages to avoid cliché, reflecting more the conventions of the genre than the historical reality. A more apt title might have been *How the Western Was Won*...

The Sons of Katie Elder (1965)

Written by: William H Wright, Allen Weiss and Harry Essex

Plot: The four sons of Katie Elder return home for their mother's funeral. John (John Wayne) is a gunfighter; Tom (Dean Martin) is a gambler; Matt (Earl Holliman) is the quiet type; and the youngest, Bud (Michael Anderson Jr.), is a student. Their mother died poor and their father was killed the same night, having lost their home in a card game. They attempt to find the men who killed their father and have to fight over ownership of their land.

Comments: Strong, powerful performances in all the main roles in this fairly uncomplicated western that conforms to the genre's stereotypes; it's always quite clear who are the 'goodies' and 'baddies'.

Nevada Smith (1966)

Written by: John Michael Hayes

Plot: A young man of mixed race, Max Sand (Steve McQueen), discovers that both his parents have been brutally murdered by three men, Bill Bowdre (Arthur Kennedy), Tom Fitch (Karl Malden) and Jesse Coe (Martin Landau). He trains as a gunsmith with an expert, Jonas Cord (Brian Keith), changes his name to Nevada Smith and sets out to find his parents' killers.

Comments: The film has an uneven pace, at times slow and at others tense and compelling. McQueen doesn't really look convincing as a man who is supposed to be half Indian. The story is based loosely on the plot of Harold Robbins' novel 'The Carpetbaggers', and its strength is in its depiction of the growing obsession of a young man who has suffered traumatic loss.

5 Card Stud (1968)

Written by: Marguerite Roberts

Plot: Five men playing poker are killed one by one. The first death seems straightforward enough, as the man is caught out cheating at cards and hanged by the others. The second is suffocated in a barrel of flour, the third is garrotted with barbed wire, the fourth hanged from the bell rope in a church and the fifth strangled. The only player not present at the hanging (Dean Martin) attempts to solve the crime. One suspect is a mysterious priest, the Rev. Jonathan Rudd (Robert Mitchum), who has recently arrived in the town.

Comments: The film is of interest for its unusual plot, and is in fact a whodunit in western costume. Hardly thought-provoking, or difficult to guess who the perpetrator is, but it is an entertaining film.

True Grit (1969)

Written by: Marguerite Roberts

Plot: Mattie Ross (Kim Darby) wants to avenge the murder of her father. She persuades Marshal Reuben 'Rooster' Cogburn (John Wayne) to help her. He has several weaknesses, however: his age, weight and a fondness for the bottle. A Texas Ranger, LaBoeuf (Glen Campbell), also helps them. They find themselves up against Ned Pepper (Robert Duvall) and his gang as well as the murderer Tom Chaney (Jeff Corey).

Comments: John Wayne finally turned in the performance which earned him an Oscar®, and his larger than life character certainly dominates the whole film. He is a lovable old rogue with a heart of gold, and the final sequences of the film are painfully moving.

Shoot Out (1971)

Written by: Marguerite Roberts

Plot: Clay Lomax (Gregory Peck) is let out of prison after a six-year sentence and determined to take revenge on his former partner, Sam Foley (James Gregory), for betraying him. However, when Clay tries to get some money from his ex-lover, he finds out that she is dead and has left behind a young girl, who is probably his daughter. Under her influence he gradually loses his sense of bitterness and resentment.

Comments: A rather sentimental film based on the novel 'Lone Cowboy' by Will James, which had been made into a film previously in black anc white in 1934 with Jackie Cooper and directed by Paul Sloane. There is more intimate dialogue than action in Hathaway's version.

HOWARD HAWKS

b. 1896. d. 1977

The career of Howard Hawks spanned the history of American cinema, from the early days of silent films, through the era of the talkies to the early 1970s. All his life he enjoyed taking risks, and even as a teenager he was racing airplanes and cars. In Hollywood he held a large variety of jobs before directing his first film. Apart from his westerns, Hawks directed some of Hollywood's all-time great films, such as *Scarface* (1932), *To Have and Have Not* (1944), *The Big Sleep* (1946), *Gentlemen Prefer Blondes* (1953), and so on. He was renowned for a rapid staccato style of dialogue in his films, in which actors often overlapped each other when speaking. He also encouraged his actors to improvise in a period when this was uncommon. While Ford's *Stagecoach* (1939) made a star of John Wayne, it was Hawks' *Red River* (1948) which established him as a powerful actor. Hawks' films reveal certain recurring themes which he never tired of investigating: group psychology, male friendship (sometimes involving an undercurrent of homo-eroticism), the need perceived as feminine for security and permanence, and the longings of men for freedom and independence. One western that is sometimes credited to him, but was finally directed by Jack Conway, is the fictionalised biography of the revolutionary Mexican general Pancho Villa, entitled *Viva Villa!* (1934). Initially the director, Hawks was fired after he refused to testify against the actor Lee Tracy, who got drunk on location in Mexico and urinated from his hotel balcony onto a passing military parade.

Barbary Coast (1935)

B&W.
Written by: Ben Hecht and Charles MacArthur

Plot: Mary Rutledge (Miriam Hopkins), arriving in California in the 1850s from the east, gets a job working in a gambling house with a corrupt boss, Luis Chamalis (Edward G Robinson). She rejects the advances of her boss for an honest young miner, Jim Carmichael (Joel McCrea), and arouses Chamalis' jealousy.

Comments: Events are based loosely on historical facts, with the character of Luis Chamalis inspired by underworld boss Charles Cora. A group of San Francisco citizens decided to form a vigilante group to clear up the criminal elements in their society, and in the film the leader of this group is called Jed Slocum (Harry Carey). In his autobiography *The Moon's a Balloon*, the actor David Niven claims that he can be spotted in a bit part as a drunken Cockney sailor coming out of a saloon.

The Outlaw (1943)

B&W.
Written by: Jules Furthman

Plot: Doc Holliday (Walter Huston) arrives in Lincoln, New Mexico, where he is greeted by his old friend Pat Garrett (Thomas Mitchell). Holliday has had his horse stolen by a stranger, who turns out to be Billy the Kid (Jack Beutel). In a surprising turn of events Holliday and Billy actually become friends. Attempting to arrest Billy, Garrett wounds him with a bullet, and Doc Holliday hides him at his ranch, where he is nursed by Holliday's girlfriend, Rio (Jane Russell). Billy once killed Rio's brother in a gunfight, but now, however, Rio and Billy fall in love.

Comments: The plot of the film bears little resemblance to historical facts. Its main claim to fame is its use of blatant sexual titillation for the first time in such an extensive way in a western. Though she was a well-trained actress (with veteran theatre director Max Reinhardt), it is clear that Jane Russell's physical attributes played a significant part in getting her the job. The censors cut 20 minutes from the film and there was a delay in its cinema release. The outcries against the indecency in some sequences continued after its release, however, and the producer Howard Hughes removed it from circulation until 1947, when it was reissued with even more titillating advertising. In 1976 it was released again and categorised as suitable for general viewing, a sign of how attitudes to sexuality in films had changed. Howard Hawks was employed as the director but reportedly didn't stay the course after a dispute with Howard Hughes, who took over total control of the production, and also had a hand in the screenplay.

Red River (1948)

B&W.
Written by: Borden Chase and Charles Schnee

Plot: Tom Dunson (John Wayne) leaves a wagon train and his girlfriend to head down south to the Red River in Texas with the aim of starting his own cattle herd. He travels with a friend, Groot (Walter Brennan), and they are soon joined by a boy, Matt Garth (Mickey Kuhn), who is the sole survivor of an Indian massacre. Dunson looks after the boy and treats him like his own son. Jump to 14 years later, and Dunson is planning to take a large herd of cattle to the Missouri railhead. On the way, because of Dunson's tyrannical leadership, young Matt (now played by Montgomery Clift) takes the herd away from Dunson and heads for a different railhead. Dunson follows them full of the desire for vengeance.

Comments: A true masterpiece of the genre, with John Wayne delivering one of his finest performances, and Montgomery Clift, a convincing one despite his inexperience in cinema at this stage, and also the ways of the west. Wayne and Clift were complete opposites, politically and emotionally, and had agreed to suppress their differences for the duration of the filming; as a result, their on-screen conflicts are electrifying. The future star, Shelley Winters, can be spotted as a girl in a dance hall. The black-and-white cinematography by Russell Harlan reveals a masterly sense of composition and the musical score by Dimitri Tiomkin is moving and stirring by turns.

The Big Sky (1952)

B&W.
Written by: Dudley Nichols

Plot: Two fur traders, Jim Deakins (Kirk Douglas) and Boone Caudill (Dewey Martin), join Boone's uncle Zeb Calloway (Arthur Hunnicutt) on a fur-trading expedition along the Mississippi into the territory of the Blackfoot Indians. Unfortunately there are both friendly and unfriendly Indians around and a ruthless gang of fur traders. Deakins and Caudill find themselves in competition for the affections of an Indian princess, Teal Eye (Elizabeth Threatt).

Comments: The strain placed on male friendship, a common theme in Hawks' films, is drawn out here over 140 minutes, with inevitable longueurs. Sometimes shown in a cut 122-minute version, its impressive black-and-white cinematography manages to maintain interest.

Rio Bravo (1959)

Written by: Leigh Brackett and Jules Furthman

Plot: In a small Texas town Sheriff John T Chance (John Wayne) arrests a man, Joe Burdette (Claude Akins), for murder and puts him in jail. Burdette's brother Nathan (John Russell) gets a gang together to free him. Chance's deputies are not best equipped to help him defend the jail: one is a drunk (Dean Martin) and the other is a cripple (Walter Brennan). But help comes from unexpected quarters: a young gunman called Colorado (Ricky Nelson) and a dance-hall girl named Feathers (Angie Dickinson).

Comments: Howard Hawks disliked the image of timid townsfolk leaving the hero to fight alone in the classic *High Noon* (1952), directed by Fred Zinnemann, and in *Rio Bravo* the sheriff is supported by a small but trustworthy group. Although the film was not accorded much critical acclaim when it first appeared, many critics now regard it as a classic of the genre. With memorable music composed by Dimitri Tiomkin, Dean Martin and Ricky Nelson also show off their talents as popular singers.

El Dorado (1966)

Written by: Leigh Brackett

Plot: Cole Thornton (John Wayne), an aging gunfighter, helps an old friend, JP Harrah (Robert Mitchum), a sheriff who has turned to drink, to fight a corrupt landowner, Bart Jason (Edward Asner), and the gang supporting him. They are helped by Mississippi (James Caan), a young man who is handy with a knife but not a gun, and old jailer, Bull Harris (Arthur Hunnicutt).

Comments: Critics have commented that the storyline is basically a remake of Hawks' earlier film *Rio Bravo* (1959), but, though there are similarities in the plots, Hawks always denied it. The title derives from a poem of the same name by Edgar Allen Poe, about a knight who grows old searching for El Dorado, which is quoted in the film.

Rio Lobo (1970)

Written by: Leigh Brackett

Plot: During the Civil War, Union captain Cord McNally (John Wayne) is responsible for a gold shipment on a railway train. Confederate soldiers steal the shipment and McNally goes in search of them. After the war he meets up with two of the rebel leaders who now agree to help him find a Union traitor who was supplying secrets to the rebel cause. In the town of Rio Lobo they find a gang of outlaws led by the man McNally has been looking for.

Comments: The three Hawks films Rio Bravo, El Dorado and Rio Lobo feature similar central scenes: a group of principled men holding on to a prisoner while being besieged. There are, however, many differences of plot and character development to make them quite distinct. This was the last film made by Howard Hawks.

HENRY KING

b.1886. d. 1982.

Well known as a director, King was also instrumental, with 35 others, in setting up the Academy of Motion Picture Arts and Sciences, which established the Oscar® award system. Westerns did not make up the highest percentage of the films he directed. He made 30 comedies and 24 romances. Of the 12 westerns he made as director, many were shorts from the silent era. The first to gain him some critical acclaim was The Winning of Barbara Worth (1926) (See chapter 4 on The Silent Westerns).

In Old Chicago (1937)

B&W.
Written by: Sonya Levien and Lamar Trotti

Plot: The film tells the story of the great fire in Chicago in 1871, focusing on the two sons of Mrs O'Leary, whose cow is reputed to have started the fire. One son is unreliable and unprincipled (Tyrone Power), and the other is a lawyer (Don Ameche).

Comments: Though set in Chicago, the film is in spirit a western, reflecting many of the genre's traditional family conflicts, and the costumes are all those found in western films. Corrupt business dealings and some musical numbers are also thrown in for good measure. The presence of the cow also lends some credence to its cla m to be a western. The 20-minute fire sequence near the end of the film cost the studio $150,000 and made it one of the most expensive films of the period.

Jesse James (1939)

Written by: Nunnally Johnson

Plot: Jesse James (Tyrone Power) returns home after the Civil War and tries to live peacefully as a farmer. His land is stolen away from him by unscrupulous bankers and railroad bosses and his mother is killed, and he and his brother Frank (Henry Fonda) find themselves forced into a life of crime, becoming famous as outlaws robbing trains.

Comments: The film sticks to the basic historical facts but greatly romanticises the character of Jesse James, making him handsome, charming and devoted to his mother. It enhances and confirms the popular image of him as a Robin Hood figure. It was made with an enormous budget for the time and became a great success at the box office. It helped to establish Henry Fonda's reputation as a powerful, sensitive performer. If you look carefully you can spot Lon Chaney Jr. as a member of the James gang.

The Gunfighter (1950)

B&W.
Written by: William Sellers and William Bowers

Plot: A gunfighter of advancing years, Jimmy Ringo (Gregory Peck), arrives in a small town, hoping to escape from his past and settle down. However, many people want to enhance their reputations by killing the famous gunfighter. Just after having come to some reconciliation with

Peggy (Helen Westcott), his estranged wife, and with some hope for the future, he is killed by a much younger man, who finds that he is now the one being hunted.

Comments: Despite not doing well at the box office on its original release, *The Gunfighter* can now be regarded as a landmark in the development of the genre. It was the first serious study of the older outlaw who tries to escape his past but cannot. Despite its inevitable ending, or perhaps because of it, the audience's sympathies are entirely with the anti-hero, who is portrayed in considerable psychological depth by Gregory Peck. The film also includes some delightfully humorous scenes of the local townspeople who are concerned to save their own skins.

The Bravados (1958)

Written by: Philip Yordan

Plot: A stranger, Jim Douglass (Gregory Peck), arrives in a town to witness the hangings of four men, the bravados of the title, for the rape and murder of his wife. They escape and he determines to hunt for them. He manages to kill three, but when he catches up with the last one he discovers that these men had nothing to do with his wife's death.

Comments: The film provides an intriguing ironic twist to the conventional revenge theme. Gregory Peck is ideally suited to the role of the silent obsessive revenger, and while our sympathies are with him at first, there is ambiguity in the film's final moments.

ANTHONY MANN

b. 1906. d. 1967.

Born in San Diego of German parents, and with the birth name of Emil Anton Bundesmann, he made altogether 42 films in various genres, including crime, history, war and romance. The largest category can be classed generally as dramas, combining elements of history, war and romance, and the most internationally well known of these are probably *The Glenn Miller Story* (1953), *El Cid* (1961) and *The Fall of the Roman Empire* (1964) The next largest group is made up of westerns, of which he made 11. Most are notable contributions to the genre, particularly the five he made with James Stewart. He himself was reputedly dissatisfied with his last western, *Cimarron* (1960).

Winchester '73 (1950)

B&W.
Written by: Borden Chase and Robert L Richards

Plot: Lin McAdam (James Stewart) is looking for the man who killed his father, and arrives in Dodge City, where a shooting contest is taking place; the prize is a celebrated repeating rifle, the Winchester '73. McAdam is awarded the rifle, but Dutch Henry (Stephen McNally) and his men rob him of it. The story then follows the fate of the rifle as it passes from one person to another: an arms dealer (John McIntire), an aggressive young Indian brave, Young Bull (Rock Hudson), a coward (Charles Drake), and an outlaw, Waco Johnnie Dean (Dan Duryea). Lola Manners (Shelley Winters), a woman of no very strict principles, tags along with whoever happens to have the gun. Only near the end of the film does McAdam find out that the man who killed his father was none other than Dutch Henry, who also happens to be his brother.

Comments: This was not only James Stewart's first western but also the first of a series he was to make with Anthony Mann. Audiences and critics alike were shocked by sequences in which Stewart revealed bitter hatred. His screen persona hitherto had been associated with a mild-mannered gentleness. He went on to make a series of westerns with the same director. Fritz Lang was originally to direct the film, and Anthony Mann only stepped in when Lang withdrew.

The Furies (1950)

B&W.
Written by: Charles Schnee

Plot: A cattle baron, TC Jeffords (Walter Huston), owns a large area of land in New Mexico known as 'The Furies'. When he decides to marry a woman from Washington, Flo Burnett (Judith Anderson), his daughter Vance (Barbara Stanwyck) reacts violently towards the woman. He banishes her from his land. He finally turns his daughter against him completely by hanging her former lover Juan Herrera (Gilbert Roland). Vance plots revenge with the aid of a gambler, Rip Darrow (Wendell Corey).

Comments: Critics have been divided over the film, viewing it as a disturbing drama utilising motifs from Greek tragedy, or a rather heavy-handed melodrama. Walter Huston puts in a fine performance, and died shortly after completion of the film.

Devil's Doorway (1950)

B&W.
Written by: Guy Trosper

Plot: A Shoshone Indian, Lance Poole (Robert Taylor), wins the Congressional Medal of Honour while fighting on the side of the Union Army at Gettysburg. He returns to his tribal lands in Wyoming to settle down as a farmer, but finds that some white men are trying to take over the land for sheep farming.

Comments: This was one of very few westerns of the time which dealt frankly with the conflicts between the Indians and the white settlers. Robert Taylor's performance, with darkened skin, as the Indian has been criticised for its lack of conviction, but Louis Calhern is impressive as the lawyer, Verne Coolan, who hates Indians. Reportedly based on the real experiences of Chief Joseph of the Nez Perce Indians.

Bend of the River (1952)

Written by: Borden Chase

Plot: A former border raider gone straight, Glyn McLyntock (James Stewart), saves Emerson Cole (Arthur Kennedy) from hanging. In the town of Portland they take on the job of leading a supply wagon train to the Columbia River area of Oregon, but a gold strike near Portland gives Cole the idea of selling the supplies to the miners at inflated prices. McLyntock is determined to ensure that the Oregon farmers get their supplies.

Comments: The second film that James Stewart made with Anthony Mann, it established his new hard-nosed persona, and, though he has a bad past, his character comes to be on the side of justice.

The Naked Spur (1953)

Written by: Sam Rolfe and Harold Jack Bloom

Plot: After his wife leaves him, having sold off his ranch while he was in the army, Howard Kemp (James Stewart) becomes a bounty hunter and sets off towards the Rockies in search of a notorious murderer, Ben Vandergroat (Robert Ryan), and to claim the $5,000 reward for his capture. He teams up with an old miner and a soldier who has been discharged.

Comments: The film has many qualities to recommend it. Shot almost entirely on location, with very impressive colour cinematography by William Mellor, all the main actors deliver decent, sensitive performances.

The Far Country (1954)

Written by: Borden Chase

Plot: It is 1896, the time of the Klondike gold rush. Jeff Webster (James

Stewart) and his partner Ben Tatum (Walter Brennan) are taking a herd of cattle to Alaska. After some hindrance by a corrupt sheriff (John McIntire) in Skagway they manage to get to Dawson. There they encounter further corruption when they sell the herd to a group of local men, who are trying to control the whole area. Ben is killed and Webster is drawn into helping the local people fight the corrupt landowners.

Comments: Greatly praised by critics and public alike for its compelling action, sensitive acting and breathtaking landscapes, shot in authentic northern ice fields. The character of the mining townships is particularly well captured.

The Man from Laramie (1955)

Written by: Philip Yordan and Frank Burt

Plot: Will Lockhart (James Stewart) is an army officer trying to find out who has been selling guns to the Apache Indians. His own brother was killed by one of these guns. He also becomes involved in a feud between two ranch owners, Kate Canaday (Aline MacMahon) and Alec Waggoman (Donald Crisp). Waggoman's son and foreman turn out to be the gunrunners. The foreman (Arthur Kennedy) kills the son and frames Lockhart for the murder.

Comments: The final collaboration between Anthony Mann and James Stewart, who considered it one of his favourite westerns. One disturbingly violent scene occurs when Lockhart is shot in the hand; the title song from the film became a popular hit at the time. (See also Chapter 6)

The Last Frontier (1955)

Written by: Russell S Hughes and Philip Yordan

Plot: An army fort is besieged by Indians, but it is unlikely that relief forces will arrive before the spring. A rather rough and ready trapper and army scout, Jed Cooper (Victor Mature), is attracted to the wife (Anne Bancroft) of the cruel commanding officer (Robert Preston) of the fort.

Comments: Mann and Mature might not have had the same chemistry as Mann and James Stewart, but the director did manage to coax one of his better performances out of Victor Mature for this film.

The Tin Star (1957)

B&W
Written by: Dudley Nichols

Plot: An ex-sheriff who has become a bounty hunter, Morg Hickman (Henry Fonda), arrives in a town, where the sheriff has recently been killed. A young inexperienced man, Ben Owens (Anthony Perkins), has taken on the job temporarily. Hickman agrees to advise the young man on the rudiments of law and order. At the climax, when the young man must face the brutal Bart Bogardus, Hickman realises that he must let the younger man stand alone.

Comments: Psychology is more important than action in a film that has been greatly praised for its two central performances by Fonda and Perkins.

Man of the West (1958)

Written by: Reginald Rose

Plot: A man who was once an outlaw, Link Jones (Gary Cooper) has married and settled down. He is entrusted with the task of finding a new schoolteacher for his community. Members of his former gang rob him, and in order to protect the people travelling with him, Billie Ellis (Julie London) and Sam Beasley (Arthur O'Connell), he pretends to rejoin the gang.

Comments: The frank treatment of sexual and violent themes hampered the audience's response on its initial release, but now *Man of the West* is regarded as a classic. One scene in which Billie Ellis is forced to strip in front of the gang is particularly disturbing.

Cimarron (1960)

Written by: Arnold Schulman

Plot: The film focuses on the Cravat family, who take part in the great land rush in the Oklahoma Territory in 1889, and build up their newspaper into a business empire. Yancey Cravat (Glenn Ford) is an idealist who angers his wife by refusing to take up the post of governor, as it will mean depriving the Indians of their land and oil.

    Comments: The 1931 version of Edna Ferber's novel, directed by Wesley Ruggles, is more faithful to the novel. The executives of the film production company, MGM, panicked when location filming encountered several bad storms and they made Mann transfer the whole production to a studio. He was forced to change the script to accommodate the shift, and was subsequently utterly dissatisfied with the final film.

SAM PECKINPAH

b.1925. d. 1984.

In 1948 Peckinpah enrolled in a graduate course in theatre studies at the University of California. He got a job with Don Siegel and was given a small part in Siegel's film *The Invasion of the Body Snatchers* (1956). He established himself first as a scriptwriter for TV westerns, some of which he also directed, such as *Gunsmoke* (from 1955), *The Rifleman* (from 1958), *The Westerner* (from 1960) and *Broken Arrow* (from 1957). His first feature film was also a western called *The Deadly Companions* (1961). The first to win critical acclaim was *Ride the High Country* (1962), starring Randolph Scott and Joel McCrea, and dealt with the theme of

The Ox-Bow Incident (1943, dir William Wellman). L to R: Henry Morgan, Henry Fonda, Michael North (20th Century Fox/Photofest).

Shane (1953, dir George Stevens). Alan Ladd as Shane (Paramount Pictures/Photofest).

The Man From Laramie (1955, dir Anthony Mann). James Stewart (Columbia Pictures/Photofest).

The Searchers (1956, dir John Ford). John Wayne (Warner Bros/Photofest).

3.10 to Yuma (1957, dir Delmer Daves). L to R: Glenn Ford, Robert Emhardt, Van Heflin (Columbia Pictures/Photofest).

The Wild Bunch (1969, dir Sam Peckinpah). L to R: Ernest Borgnine and William Holden (Warner Bros/Photofest).

Silverado (1985, dir Lawrence Kasdan). L to R: Kevin Costner, Scott Glenn, Kevin Kline, Danny Glover (Columbia Pictures/Photofest).

Unforgiven (1992, dir Clint Eastwood). L to R: Clint Eastwood, Shane Meier, Aline Levasseur (Warner Bros/Photofest).

High Noon (1952, dir Fred Zinnemann). Grace Kelly and Gary Cooper (United Artists/Photofest).

The Magnificent Seven (1960, dir John Sturges). L to R: Yul Brynner, Steve McQueen, Horst Buchnolz, Charles Bronson, Robert Vaughn, Brad Dexter, James Coburn (United Artists/Photofest).

ageing gunfighters, one he would return to in one of his most well-known films, *The Wild Bunch* (1969). *Straw Dogs* (1971) stirred up public debate due to its explicit violence. Other notable westerns are *The Ballad of Cable Hogue* (1970) and *Pat Garrett and Billy the Kid* (1973). Well known amongst his non-western output are *The Getaway* (1972), *Bring Me the Head of Alfredo Garcia* (1974), which has become something of a cult film, and the road movie *Convoy* (1978), with Kris Kristofferson and Ali MacGraw.

The Deadly Companions (1961)

Written by: AS Fleischman

Plot: A woman's son is accidentally killed by an ex-army officer (Brian Keith), who goes by the name of Yellowleg, and agrees to accompany her (Maureen O'Hara) across a desert, so that the son can be buried next to his father. On the way they have to contend with the behaviour of the ex-army officer's companions (Chill Wills and Steve Cochran) and aggressive Indians.

Comments: Peckinpah's first western for the cinema after his long run of films for various TV series. The actor Brian Keith who had acted for him in *The Westerner* suggested to him that the story might work well in the cinema. The film maintains a slow pace but is constantly absorbing, with many scenes shot in close-up between the man and the woman, subtly revealing their gradual growth in intimacy. The style was undoubtedly influenced by Peckinpah's work for the small screen.

Ride the High Country (aka Guns in the Afternoon) (1962)

Written by: NB Stone Jr.

Plot: Steve Judd (Joel McCrea), a former lawman, rides into a town and mistakenly believes that the Fourth of July cheers he hears are for him.

He has been asked by some local bankers to collect some newly discovered gold in the High Sierras, but feels he may now be a little too old to undertake the job alone. He therefore asks an old friend, also a former lawman, Gil Westrum (Randolph Scott), to accompany him. Gil brings with him a young friend, Heck Longtree (Ron Starr), who handles a gun well. On the way a young girl, Elsa Knudsen (Mariette Hartley), joins them to escape from her restricted life with her father and find the man she wants to marry, Billy Hammond (James Drury). Gil and Heck plan to steal the gold.

Comments: The opening sequence is very cleverly contrived to show how the Old West is dying, with Gil dressed in a parody of an old western hero, and the modern age dawning, with shots of a car and a uniformed policeman. The main part of the film respects the traditions of the genre – Steve dies with dignity ('I'll go it alone') and Gil promises to hand the gold over to the bank – and emphasises personal responsibility and the importance of being faithful to one's values. Apparently Scott and McCrea were cast to play each other's roles, but each actor requested independently that the casting be reversed. Clearly the right decision.

Major Dundee (1965)

Written by: Harry Julian Fink, Oscar Saul and Sam Peckinpah

Plot: Near the end of the Civil War a group of Apache massacres the inhabitants of a cavalry post in New Mexico. Major Amos Dundee (Charlton Heston) is the commander of another post nearby, who decides to take revenge for the attack with a mixed band of Confederate prisoners, Union deserters and thieves. A Confederate captain, Benjamin Tyreen (Richard Harris), who is a former friend of Dundee, agrees to help him. Both men become involved with the same attractive widow (Senta Berger).

Comments: The production of the film has a rather unfortunate history, which has left it uneven in terms of quality. Two major scenes were cut against the director's will and due to Peckinpah's treatment of the actors he almost came to blows with Charlton Heston. The battle scenes are very well handled, however, and the acting is of a high calibre throughout. A restored version is now available (2005).

The Wild Bunch (1969)

Written by: Sam Peckinpah, Walon Green and Roy N Sickner

Plot: A group of ageing outlaws led by Pike Bishop (William Holden) ride into the Texas border town of San Rafael to rob a bank. The setting, however, is in 1913, when such things were very much a thing of the past. A group of mercenaries under the leadership of Deke Thornton (Robert Ryan) awaits them, and many innocent bystanders are caught in the crossfire. The Bishop gang escapes into Mexico, and find themselves in the middle of the Mexican Revolution. Bishop discovers too late that the bags they have stolen contain worthless metal and not gold. The gang does a deal with General Mapache (Emilio Fernández), an opponent of Pancho Villa, by which they are to rob a train supplying guns for the army and sell the goods to Mapache's men. Angel (Jaime Sanchez) kills the girl who was previously his lover but is now the mistress of Mapache. When Mapache discovers this he captures Angel. Pike decides to try and release Angel, but Angel is killed and a bloodbath ensues.

Comments: For a long time the qualities of this film as a fine example of western genre revisionism were overshadowed by controversy over its use of violence and gore, which proved too excessive for some. The opening slaughter of the innocent and the final confrontation, with its extensive slow-motion depiction of bloody violence, is undoubtedly sickening yet such scenes can also be seen as cathartic. A contrast to the idealisation and romanticisation of such shoot-outs in many classic westerns, the way of life during this period is depicted with convincing realism. (See also Chapter 11)

The Ballad of Cable Hogue (1970)

Written by: John Crawford and Edmund Penney

Plot: Cable Hogue (Jason Robards) is left to die in a desert, but finds water and survives. Together with a prostitute called Hildy (Stella Stevens) he starts a new life running a rest stop on a local stagecoach route. Cable is badly wounded when he is run over by a car and prefers to die outdoors rather than in a house.

Comments: The film presents another metaphor for the dying West and its ideals, but without the violence of *The Wild Bunch*, and with added nostalgia and a touch of humour.

Junior Bonner (1972)

Written by: Jeb Rosebrook

Plot: A rodeo rider, Junior Bonner (Steve McQueen), who is past his best, returns to his home in Arizona, to take part in a special 'Frontier Days Rodeo' to celebrate the 4th of July. His younger brother, Curly (Joe Don Baker), is becoming a millionaire through land development. Junior wins the prize at the rodeo and gives the money to his father, a former rodeo rider himself, to enable him to realise his dream of moving to Australia.

Comments: Along with *The Ballad of Cable Hogue* this film belies the widely held belief that Peckinpah depicted the decline of the West solely through the use of excessive violence. The character of Junior Bonner embodies that decline with a gentle dignity, making his performance at the rodeo a moving swansong.

Pat Garrett and Billy the Kid (1973)

Written by: Rudy Wurlitzer

Plot: The film tells the familiar story of the pursuit of the outlaw Billy the Kid (Kris Kristofferson) by former outlaw Pat Garrett (James Coburn) who has been made a sheriff. Garrett finally finds Billy in his house at night and kills him. More than 20 years later Garrett himself is murdered, his death ordered by the same businessmen who paid him to kill Billy.

Comments: The film contains several of Peckinpah's trademark slow-motion killings and nostalgia for a lifestyle now lost. Peckinpah himself plays a character encouraging Garrett to the final deed. Bob Dylan appears in the film as a drifter and his songs are used on the soundtrack, including the hit 'Knocking on Heaven's Door'. The film was recut on its first release without consulting Peckinpah, but editor Roger Spottswoode has restored it to a form closer to Peckinpah's original, particularly the scenes of Garrett's own death.

GEORGE STEVENS

b. 1904. d. 1975.

Stevens was born in Oakland, California, to parents who ran their own theatre company. In 1922 the family moved south to Glendale to find work in the film industry. Both parents managed to get jobs as film actors, and at the age of 17 Stevens got a job as assistant cameraman at the Hal Roach studio, where he was eventually involved in shooting low-budget westerns. He worked as cameraman on several Laurel and Hardy shorts, and the first film he directed which became a classic was the musical *Swing Time* (1936), featuring Fred Astaire and Ginger Rogers. Other successes included *Gunga Din* (1939). In World War Two he was head of the Combat Motion Picture Unit, filming the Normandy landings, the liberation of Paris and the concentration camp at Dachau, amongst other events. In 1951 his updated version of Theodore Dreiser's *An American Tragedy* appeared as *A Place in the Sun*, in which he used close-ups much more frequently than was the norm at the time. Many of Stevens' films focus on the lives of outsiders, and his most famous contribution to the western genre, *Shane* (1953), was no exception. He followed this with *Giant* (1956), based on Edna Ferber's novel about life in Texas, and went on to make *The Diary of Anne Frank* (1959), *The Greatest Story Ever Told* (1965) and *The Only Game in Town* (1970). Stevens' only other contribution to the western genre as director was *Annie Oakley* (1935).

Annie Oakley (1935)

B&W.
Written by: Joel Sayre and John Twist

Plot: In a match of sharpshooters, the manager of a hotel decides to bet on the person who has been supplying him with quail. This turns out to be Annie Oakley (Barbara Stanwyck), who is subsequently hired to perform in Buffalo Bill's Wild West Show, and trained by the champion performer Toby Walker (Preston Foster), with whom a close relationship develops. However, professional rivalry disrupts their relationship.

Comments: The film somewhat romanticises the life story of Annie Oakley, but provides a convincing re-creation of the famous Buffalo Bill's Wild West Show. Stanwyck plays Annie as an intelligent, independent woman, with whom feminists can identify, and it was the start of a long line of western heroines that she went on to play.

Shane (1953)

Written by: AB Guthrie

Plot: A stranger, Shane (Alan Ladd), arrives out of nowhere at the homestead of the Starrett family. He is dressed in buckskin and sports a fancy revolver. The young son (Brandon de Wilde) regards him with awe. Shane is drawn into the feud between the owners of small farms in the valley led by Joe Starrett (Van Heflin) and the ranchers led by Ryker (Emile Meyer) who want to possess their land. Ryker hires Wilson (Jack Palance) to threaten the farmers. Starrett's wife Marian (Jean Arthur) is clearly attracted to Shane, and pleads with him not to fight with Wilson, but Shane is determined to make the valley safe for decent people to live in.

Comments: Few westerns have attracted so many superlatives among critics as this film and deservedly so. Splendid cinematography and a stunning Wyoming landscape set against the background of the Grand Teton Mountains provide the setting for a moving story of a boy's adoration of a mysterious gunman with a heart of gold. The storyline is composed from familiar western elements – homesteaders versus ranchers, goodies versus baddies – but the human relationships at the centre of the film are developed with great subtlety and conviction, with powerful performances from all the leading actors. Alan Ladd has been universally praised, and combines, in a carefully restrained performance, reserve, dignity and strength. Even Jack Palance, with barely a dozen or so lines of dialogue, manages to add convincing menace through his black-clad villain. The drab life in the frontier town is also depicted in authentic detail. The theme music, with the title 'The Call of the Faraway Hills', became a hit as soon as it was released. (See also Chapter 6)

JOHN STURGES

b.1911. d. 1992

Sturges is famous for films dealing with serious moral and social issues as well as his westerns. Notable among his non-westerns are *Bad Day at Black Rock* (1955), which is set in 1945, but has a plot that owes much to the western genre; his powerful version of the Hemingway classic *The Old Man and the Sea* (1958); *Never So Few* (1959), about the military campaign in Burma; *The Great Escape* (1963), rated a classic wartime escape film; *Ice Station Zebra* (1968); and *The Eagle Has Landed* (1976). Sturges is also credited as co-director with Duilio Coletti on a western filmed in Italy, Spain and France, known variously as *Valdez, Il Mezzosangue*, *Valdez the Halfbreed*, and *The Valdez Horses* (1973), about a horse breeder played by Charles Bronson, and his relationship to a young protegé. The film was not widely released, however, and gained no critical recognition.

The Walking Hills (1949)

B&W.
Written by: Alan Le May

Plot: The film is set in a Mexican border town, where a group of men discover that an old wagon train which had been loaded with gold is buried somewhere in the desert. They set out in search of the gold in the company of a beautiful woman (Ella Raines), and various psychological conflicts develop.

Comments: There are strong performances from all the leading actors in this profound and sensitive film. Prominent among them are Randolph Scott and William Bishop. The blues singer Josh White features with a rendering of 'Delta Blues'.

Escape From Fort Bravo (1953)

Written by: Frank Fenton

Plot: Set in the Civil War in 1863, the film relates the story of a woman, Carla Forester (Eleanor Parker), who helps her fiancé John Marsh (John Forsythe), a Confederate officer, escape from a remote Union prison camp. She subsequently falls in love with the Union officer, Captain

Roper (William Holden), who runs a strict regime at the fort, and captured Marsh in the first place.

Comments: Featuring strong performances by the three leads, and evocative images of the desert provided by cinematographer Robert Surtees, the film was originally made in 3-D, but the popularity of this technique was already in decline and a normal version was released in cinemas.

Backlash (1956)

Written by: Borden Chase

Plot: Jim Slater (Richard Widmark) searches for the sole survivor of an ambush by Apache Indians in which his father died. The survivor was supposed to have gone to get help but absconded instead with a hoard of gold. Various people, including the widow, Karyl Orton (Donna Reed), of one of the other dead men, and the determined Walker brothers, believe that Jim already has the gold and are intent on depriving him of it. When Jim finally catches up with the survivor he has to face a shocking truth.

Comments: Based on a novel by Frank Gruber, in contrast to many westerns the focus of the film is on the intimate personal drama as opposed to the problems with the local Indians and the impending range war.

Gunfight at the OK Corral (1957)

Written by: Leon Uris

Plot: The film opens in Fort Griffith, Texas, with Wyatt Earp (Burt Lancaster) saving Doc Holliday (Kirk Douglas) from being lynched. Later they meet again in Dodge City, Kansas, and Holliday accompanies Earp to the town of Tombstone to deal with the notorious Clanton gang. This culminates in the famous shoot-out at the OK Corral.

Comments: Neither the best nor the most historically accurate of the film versions of the story, but it has proved popular with the public, especially among Lancaster and Douglas fans. The title song by Dimitri Tiomkin became a hit for the singer Frankie Laine. Sturges later made another version of the same story in *Hour of the Gun* (1967).

The Law and Jake Wade (1958)

Written by: William Bowers

Plot: The outlaw Jake Wade (Robert Taylor) wants to go straight and has settled down as a marshal, but he is dogged by his former partner, Clint Hollister (Richard Widmark), who wants to find a hoard of stolen money, the whereabouts of which is known only to Jake.

Comments: Not a remarkable film but there are sound performances all round, with Richard Widmark playing the type of loathsome psychopath he had mastered so well.

Last Train From Gun Hill (1959)

Written by: James Poe

Plot: A marshal in the town of Pauley, Matt Morgan (Kirk Douglas), is married to an Indian woman, who is raped and killed by two young men, Rick Belden (Earl Holliman) and Lee Smithers (Brian Hutton). Eventually Matt discovers that one of the killers, Rick, is the son of his old friend Craig Belden (Anthony Quinn), a cattle baron in Gun Hill. When Matt tries to take Rick back to Pauley by the last train, he is challenged by Craig and his men.

Comments: The film is notable for the suspense created as they wait for the last train to arrive, a technique already used in Fred Zinnemann's *High Noon* (1952) and Delmer Daves' *3.10 to Yuma* (1957).

The Magnificent Seven (1960)

Written by: William Roberts

Plot: A gang of bandits led by Calvera (Eli Wallach) terrorise a small Mexican town and the townspeople hire a group of gunfighters to rid them of the menace. The film follows the recruitment of the gunmen by Chris (Yul Brynner) and explores the psychology of each. Eventually the gunmen develop a real concern for the farmers and townspeople they have been employed to protect.

Comments: Based on the famous film *The Seven Samurai* (1954) by the Japanese director Akira Kurosawa, the film's real interest is in the characterisation of the seven gunmen. There is Chris the mysterious lone fighter; the man of few words Vin (Steve McQueen); the insecure young Chico (Horst Buchholz); the half-breed O'Reilly (Charles Bronson); Lee (Robert Vaughn), who's trying to regain lost courage; Britt (James Coburn), skilled at throwing knives; and Harry (Brad Dexter), hoping to find a hoard of treasure. There is much incidental philosophy in the film, especially about the nature of violence and the use of power, but its strength resides in the ways t maintains suspense and in the exploration of conflicts between the main characters. The theme music by Elmer Bernstein was nominated for an Oscar® and has retained its popularity ever since.

Sergeants 3 (1962)

Written by: WR Burnett

Plot: Set in the West after the Civil War, the film is about a freed slave, Jonah Williams (Sammy Davis Jr.), who joins up with three sergeants and helps them become heroes when Indians attack a group of settlers.

Comments: A comedy western version of the poem 'Gunga Din' by Rudyard Kipling, which serves mainly as a vehicle for Frank Sinatra and his famous 'rat pack': Dean Martin, Sammy Davis, Peter Lawford and others. The film retains its popularity but is hardly a memorable contribution to the genre.

The Hallelujah Trail (1965)

Written by: John Gay

Plot: A shipment of whisky is being taken to miners in Denver with a guard of cavalry under the leadership of Colonel Thaddeus Gearhart (Burt Lancaster) and Captain Paul Slater (Jim Hutton). The cavalry has to contend with Indian tribes, and the female leader of a local temperance society, Cora Templeton Massingale (Lee Remick), not to mention some of the cavalry itself who are keen to get their hands on the tempting cargo.

Comments: Based on a novel by Bill Gulick, this comedy western is certainly enjoyable and amusing, though several jokes begin to wear a little thin over the course of a very long film. There is a particularly hilarious performance by Martin Landau as an Indian chief with the name Chief-Walks-Stooped-Over, who is determined to get hold of the whisky at all costs.

Hour of the Gun (1967)

Written by: Edward Anhalt

Plot: The story begins with the famous gunfight at the OK Corral and recounts the attempt by Wyatt Earp (James Garner) to take revenge for the death of his brother. He becomes more concerned with this mission than with his responsibilities to maintain law and order in the town of Tombstone.

Comments: This is essentially a sequel to Sturges' famous film *Gunfight at the OK Corral* (1957). James Garner imbues Earp with an obsessive character, and it is Doc Holliday (Jason Robards) who represents the moral conscience of the film.

Joe Kidd (1972)

Written by: Elmore Leonard

Plot: The film is set in Mexico. Joe Kidd (Clint Eastwood), a former bounty hunter, is hired by the big landowner Frank Harlan (Robert Duvall) to find the Mexican revolutionary Luis Chama (John Saxon), who is helping Mexicans to claim land in the US which is rightfully theirs. However, Kidd eventually becomes convinced that Harlan is the real villain and becomes part of a range war against him.

Comments: Not one of Eastwood's best performances, but Robert Duvall is compelling as the vicious Harlan. The climax involving a locomotive being driven off the rails is stunning.

KING VIDOR

b.1894. d. 1982

As a child he survived the worst hurricane to ever hit America at that time, devastating the whole town of Galveston, in Texas, in 1900. It inspired his first film, the black-and-white and silent *Hurricane in Galveston* in 1913. Throughout his career he not only directed but also wrote many screenplays and stories that were made into screenplays. He has been registered in the Guinness Book of World Records as the man with the longest career as film director, spanning 67 years from 1913 to 1980, and is credited with the insight: 'In Hollywood the cameraman lights the star. In Europe he lights the set.'

Billy the Kid (1930)

B&W.
Written by: Charles MacArthur, Laurence Stallings and Wanda Tuchock

Plot: Billy the Kid (Johnny Mack Brown) murders a land baron William Donovan (James Marcus) in revenge for the murder of a friend. Billy and his bride are pursued by Sheriff Pat Garrett (Wallace Beery). There are two alternative endings for the film: an historically inaccurate one for the American audience, in which Garrett allows Billy to escape over the border into Mexico; and the historically accurate one for European audiences, in which Garrett kills Billy.

  Comments: This was the first sound version of the story of Billy the Kid and based on the novel *Saga of Billy the Kid* (1927) by Walter Noble Burns. It has been praised for its realism. Both cast and sets have a worn, grubby look, and Vidor shot most of the scenes in areas of New Mexico where Billy the Kid spent much of his time. William S Hart loaned the production a gun said to have been used by the real Billy the Kid.

The Texas Rangers (1936)

B&W.
Written by: Louis Stevens

Plot: Three outlaw friends are separated after committing a robbery. Jim Hawkins (Fred MacMurray) and Wahoo Jones (Jack Oakie) realise the error of their ways and become Texas Rangers, while the third, Sam McGee (Lloyd Nolan), continues his career as an outlaw. Hawkins and Jones set out to bring McGee to justice.

  Comments: While based on the book *The Texas Rangers* by Walter Prescott Webb, the story was actually written by Vidor himself. Notable is a cameo role by George 'Gabby' Hayes as a judge. The film was remade in 1949 under the title *Streets of Laredo*, with William Holden,

William Bendix and Macdonald Carey, but directed by Leslie Fenton, with Vidor credited as one of the screenplay writers. It is generally not rated so highly as the original, however. There is another film, made in 1951, also called *The Texas Rangers* and directed by Phil Karlson, with a basic plot which is remarkably similar.

Northwest Passage (1940)

Written by: Talbot Jennings and Laurence Stallings

Plot: The story is set in colonial America during the French and Indian War (1754–63) and based on historical events. Major Robert Rogers (Spencer Tracy) is the commander of the famous 'Rogers' Rangers'. Rogers has plans to seek the famed Northwest Passage, a route through the Canadian Arctic from the Atlantic to the Pacific, once the war is over, but the film mainly recounts the story of a group of the rangers sent to quell some Indians who are helping the enemy.

Comments: The film was nominated for an Oscar® for Best Colour Cinematography, and the landscapes are stunning. It must be stressed that this was the first part of an intended two-part film, so that the actual search for the Northwest Passage does not feature in this first part. For complex reasons, partly financial, the second part was never made. The historical Rogers never fulfilled his dream.

Duel in the Sun (1946)

Written by: David O'Selznick, and others

Plot: Half-breed Pearl Chavez (Jennifer Jones) goes to live with distant relatives in Texas when her father (Herbert Marshall) is hanged for shooting his wife and her lover. She becomes involved with the family of a cattle rancher, Senator Jackson McCanles (Lionel Barrymore), who has two sons of completely contrasting characters: Jesse (Joseph Cotten) is upright and honest, while Lewton, known as Lewt (Gregory Peck), is arrogant and unprincipled. Pearl is attracted to Lewt, but a rancher, Sam Pierce (Charles Bickford), is also attracted to her. Violence breaks the triangle.

Comments: King Vidor is credited as the sole director, but left the production after disagreements with the producer David O. Selznick. Various other directors are known to have contributed scenes, including Selznick himself, and also Otto Brower, William Dieterle, Josef von Sternberg, Sidney Franklin and William Cameron Menzies. The screenplay was written by Selznick too, based on an adaptation by Oliver HP Garrett of a novel by Niven Busch, and Ben Hecht is also known to have had a hand in the writing. One can readily understand why Vidor wanted to quit the production, with Selznick attempting to dominate all aspects. With Jennifer Jones his lover and soon to become his wife, Selznick was determined that her role in the film be as prominent as possible. It caused a stir at the time for its strong sexual imagery and the passionate intensity of its embraces.

Man Without a Star (1955)

Written by: Borden Chase and DD Beauchamp

Plot: A drifter, Dempsey Rae (Kirk Douglas), befriends young, inexperienced Jeff Jimson (William Campbell), and both get work for a woman rancher, Reed Bowman (Jeanne Crain). Dempsey becomes emotionally involved with Reed, but when she indulges in dishonest dealing he leaves her to side with the local ranchers. Reed employs the brutal Steve Miles to take over Dempsey's job, and the two meet in violent conflict.

Comments: The film has been praised for Kirk Douglas's performance. It is not surprising that he put a lot of effort into it, as it was one of the first films to be made by his own production company. He also performs a little party piece, singing with a banjo.

RAOUL WALSH

b. 1837. d. 1980.

Walsh's career as a director spans 52 years. He learned his craft and production management techniques working as assistant director with DW Griffith on *The Clansman*, which became better known as *The Birth of a Nation* (1915). In the same year he wrote and directed his own first feature-length film, *Regeneration*. From 1914 to 1917 he directed a few short westerns, such as *Out of the Deputy's Hands* (1914), *A Bad Man and Others* (1915), *Blue Blood and Red* (1916) and *The Conqueror* (1917), but it was with the first sound film made outdoors, *In Old Arizona* (1928), that he made his first notable western. In the course of his career he made films in a large variety of genres, and those for which he is particularly remembered are *The Roaring Twenties* (1939), *High Sierra* (1941) and *Strawberry Blonde* (1941) among others. He also directed James Cagney in one of his most enduring performances in the classic crime film *White Heat* (1949). In a state of severe ill health he directed a powerful version of Norman Mailer's *The Naked and the Dead* (1958), an unflinching analysis of the relationships between soldiers in a war.

In Old Arizona (1928)

B&W.
Written by: Tom Barry

Plot: An attractive Mexican woman, Tonia (Dorothy Burgess), finds herself caught in a love triangle with the handsome outlaw, the Cisco Kid (Warner Baxter), and a Texas Ranger, Mickey Dunn (Edmund Lowe), who is chasing him.

Comments: Based on the short story 'The Caballero's Way' by O Henry (William Sydney Porter) this was the first noteworthy sound western, and the first to employ sound recording equipment successfully outside the soundproofed world of the studio. The film is long by contemporary standards and slowly paced, but Warner Baxter is convincing in the lead role. Although many of the actors appear insecure in handling dialogue in the new, unfamiliar medium of sound, the novelty of outdoor sound recording made it a surefire hit on its release. Some sequences, which were clearly added to provide opportunities to show off the sound system, such as the mariachi band who appear from nowhere to play a song, hold up the action. The sound that most amazed the film's first audiences, however, was that of bacon frying in a pan.

There is a fascinating story of an incident which occurred during the making of this film which affected its casting and left Raoul Walsh scarred for life. While returning from location shooting in Utah, Walsh had an accident: a jackrabbit jumped against the windscreen of his car and he was blinded in one eye. For the rest of his life he had to wear an eye patch. He had planned to play the role of the Cisco Kid himself, but as a result of his injury Warner Baxter played the role and Walsh handed over much of the direction to Irving Cummings. Baxter was immediately popular with audiences and went on to play the role in two sequels: *The Cisco Kid* (1931), also directed by Irving Cummings, and *The Return of the Cisco Kid* (1939), directed by Herbert Leeds.

The Big Trail (1930)

B&W.
Written by: Marie Boyle, Jack Peabody and Florence Postal

Plot: Breck Coleman (John Wayne) is the scout of a wagon train going west from Missouri to Oregon. He becomes romantically involved with Ruth (Marguerite Churchill). She is also pursued by Thorpe (Ian Keith), who claims to own a plantation but in fact survives on his gambling. Breck is trying to find the men who murdered a friend of his, and starts to suspect that they are the leaders of the wagon train, Flack (Tyrone Power) and Lopez (Charles Stevens).

Comments: The film is most notable for its stunning visual sequences and for providing John Wayne with his first starring role. He has a youthful charm but lacks the self-confidence of his mature performances. It was John Ford who recommended the 23-year-old Duke Morrison, as he then styled himself, and whose full name was Marion Michael Morrison. When he needed to find a more American sounding name, Walsh suggested 'Anthony Wayne', but they eventually settled on 'John'. It was to Walsh that John Wayne owed the training he received in basic cowboy skills, such as mounting and riding a horse, and drawing a gun.

The film's action sequences are justly renowned: shots of the enormously long wagon train pulled by oxen, a buffalo hunt, a snowstorm, an extensive Indian attack and, most stunning of all, a sequence in which the entire wagon train, together with its oxen, is lowered down a steep cliff. While the film won critical acclaim, it was not a box-office success; not many cinemas at the time were equipped to show it in the 70mm wide-screen version (with the so-called 'Grandeur' process), and screened it instead in a shortened 35mm version.

Dark Command (1940)

B&W.
Written by: F Hugh Herbert, Lionel Houser, and Grover Jones

Plot: In the township of Lawrence, Kansas, shortly before the Civil War, a schoolteacher, Will Cantrell (Walter Pidgeon), seeks election as a federal marshal but is beaten by a cowboy, Bob Seton (John Wayne). Cantrell also discovers that Seton is pursuing the girl whom he loves, Mary McCloud (Claire Trevor). When Seton has to put Mary's brother Fletch (Roy Rogers) on trial for murder, Cantrell takes advantage of the situation to win Mary's affections, and corrupts the jury with threats of violence. On being set free Fletch joins the gang of outlaws run by Cantrell.

Comments: Based on a novel by WR Burnett, which was itself inspired by the real-life story of the Quantrill Raiders. The shoot-out scenes are excitingly staged and the burning down of the town has lost none of its effectiveness with the passage of time. Victor Young's musical score is appropriately stirring.

They Died with Their Boots On (1941)

B&W.
Written by: Wally Kline and Aeneas MacKenzie

Plot: The film traces the life of George Custer (Errol Flynn) from his time as cadet at West Point to his participation in the Civil War and his death at the Battle of Little Bighorn, reflecting also his relationship with wife Libby Bacon Custer (Olivia de Havilland).

Comments: Errol Flynn's portrayal of Custer is in the noble, swash-buckling mould that he so effectively made his own, bearing none of the negative traits that have since been imputed to the historical general. Here Custer is depicted as a defender of the rights of the Indians against the machinations of unscrupulous businessmen. There are notable performances by Anthony Quinn as Chief Crazy Horse, one of the multifarious ethnic roles he was to become famous for, and by Sidney Greenstreet as General Winfield Scott. This was the last of the eight films that Flynn and de Havilland made together.

Pursued (1947)

B&W.
Written by: Niven Busch

Plot: A Civil War veteran is haunted by an unknown event from the past, the nature of which is gradually revealed. There has been a feud between two families, the Callums and the Rands. Medora Callum

(Judith Anderson) had an affair with the father of Jeb Rand (Robert Mitchum), and in revenge Grant Callum (Dean Jagger) killed all the other members of Jeb's family. Jeb develops a passion for his stepsister, Thorley Callum (Teresa Wright), and kills her brother in a gunfight. She agrees to marry him, but only so that she can avenge her brother's death.

Comments: Robert Mitchum and Teresa Wright provide strong natural performances and lend conviction to the melodramatic storyline. For its gradual unravelling of a dark mystery and its psychological depth this film can be aptly described as a noir western. The film helped Robert Mitchum establish his popularity as a rugged, broody hero.

Cheyenne (aka *The Wyoming Kid*) (1947)

B&W.
Written by: Alan Le May, Paul Wellman and Thames Williamson

Plot: A gambler called James Wylie (Dennis Morgan) is caught by a sheriff who gives him the option of returning to face a trial or assist in tracking down a notorious outlaw known as 'The Poet' who has been robbing Wells Fargo stagecoaches. He decides to take his chances and help find the outlaw, and rides on one of the stagecoaches together with two women, Emily (Janis Paige) and Ann (Jane Wyman), only to find that Ann is the wife of the very outlaw he is seeking.

Comments: The storyline develops episodically, registering unexpected changes of mood, from danger and excitement, to sexual flirtation and comedy. The contrasting characters of the two women are well developed and unusually complex. The gunfight at the film's climax is impressively staged.

Silver River (1948)

B&W.
Written by: Stephen Longstreet and Harriet Frank Jr.

Plot: Mike McComb (Errol Flynn) is unjustly discharged from the cavalry and sets out for Nevada, where he establishes himself, through ruthless means, as one of the most powerful silver magnates. He even resorts to having one of his men sent to his death so that he can marry his wife. Eventually, other mining companies turn against him and even his wife and friends desert him.

Comments: Most of the exciting action sequences occur in the first ten minutes or so, and the pace never really picks up again. At the time of its release fans of Errol Flynn's popular 'idealistic swashbuckling hero' film persona were greatly disappointed to see him as an unprincipled seeker of power and wealth. It was the last time that Errol Flynn and Raoul Walsh worked together.

Colorado Territory (1949)

B&W.
Written by: Edmund H North and John Twist

Plot: An outlaw, Wes McQueen (Joel McCrea), is set free from jail by his gang and meets Julie Ann (Dorothy Malone), who inspires him to seek a better life. He decides to attempt one last robbery to ensure a better future for himself, but Julie Ann betrays him and he finds the train he plans to rob full of lawmen. He flees in the company of a half-breed woman friend, Colorado Carson (Virginia Mayo), to the mountains, but they can find no escape.

Comments: The film is a remake in the western idiom of the famous Raoul Walsh film *High Sierra* (1941), which was in turn based on the novel by WR Burnett. Walsh's use of the landscape is more accomplished in the later film, and the ultimate fate of the protagonists strikes a grimmer note.

Along the Great Divide (aka The Travelers) **(1951)**

Written by: Walter Doniger and Lewis Meltzer

Plot: The Rodens are pursuing an old man, Tim Keith (Walter Brennan), who they believe killed one of their family. A new federal marshal, Len Merrick (Kirk Douglas), prevents them from hanging the man they suspect and insists on bringing him to trial in Santa Loma. The Rodens are intent upon a hanging, however, and Merrick attempts to escape from them with the old man and his daughter (Virginia Mayo) via a desert route.

Comments: Kirk Douglas's first western, the film contains consistently engaging central performances and a memorable cameo from John Agar as the deputy Billy Shear. On occasion, the landscape shots are breathtaking.

Distant Drums **(1951)**

Written by: Martin Rackin and Niven Busch

Plot: Captain Quincy Wyatt (Gary Cooper) leads a small group of men into the Florida Everglades to suppress an uprising of Seminole Indians. In the course of their journey they are joined by a beautiful girl, Judy Beckett (Mari Aldon), and her servant.

Comments: Romance drives this film, which features the beautiful, natural environment of the Florida Everglades, an evocative musical score, haunting drumbeats and subtle acting from Gary Cooper.

The Lawless Breed (1952)

Written by: Bernard Gordon

Plot: John Wesley Hardin (Rock Hudson), a famous gunman, returns home after 16 years in prison to find that he is worshipped by his teenage son, who wishes to follow in his footsteps. With the express intention of showing his son the dangers of such a lifestyle he deliberately joins a gang and sacrifices himself for the sake of his son's future.

Comments: Based on the story of the historical Hardin, using his own account that was published after his release from prison, the film unjustly depicts him as a sympathetic figure, opting for a sentimental ending. It marks the first time Rock Hudson was given top billing.

Gun Fury (1953)

Written by: Roy Huggins and Irving Wallace

Plot: Ben Warren (Rock Hudson) hates violence, but when his fiancée, Jennifer Ballard (Donna Reed), is abducted by a gang of outlaws, he is stirred to seek revenge on the leader of the gang, Frank Slayton (Philip Carey).

Comments: Originally made in 3-D, the film helped to establish Rock Hudson as a major star.

Saskatchewan (aka O'Rourke of the Royal Mounted) (1954)

Written by: Gil Doud

Plot: While returning home from duty at an outpost, Inspector O'Rourke of the Canadian Mounted Police (Alan Ladd) and his Cree Indian half-brother Cajou (Jay Silverheels) rescue an American girl, Grace Markey (Shelley Winters), from an Indian attack on a wagon train. He takes her to Fort Saskatchewan but then discovers that she is being sought by a US marshal, Carl Smith (Hugh O'Brian). O'Rourke risks court martial when he decides not to hand the girl over to the marshal. With an uprising of Sioux Indians, it becomes necessary to leave the fort and undertake a long journey, fraught with dangers, to Fort Walsh.

Comments: Memorable for its depiction of the differences between the Canadian and American attitudes towards the native Indian populations. The brilliant cinematography by John F Seitz provides stunning views of the Canadian Rockies.

The Tall Men (1955)

Written by: Sydney Boehm and Frank S Nugent

Plot: Two brothers, Ben Allison (Clark Gable) and Clint Allison (Cameron Mitchell), ex-soldiers of the Confederate army, travel to Montana in the hope of making their fortune in the gold fields. They end up working for the unscrupulous Nathan Stark (Robert Ryan), helping him drive a herd of cattle. On their way, they rescue a beautiful woman, Nella Turner (Jane Russell), from attacking Indians. Ben and Stark subsequently find themselves vying for her attentions.

Comments: Suffering from a lacklustre storyline, this is hardly the most compelling of westerns. Its main attractions are a star-studded cast, in particular Jane Russell, and the glamorous Technicolor cinematography.

The King and Four Queens (1956)

Written by: Richard Allen Simmons and Margaret Fitts

Plot: A cowboy, Dan Kehoe (Clark Gable), has heard that a hoard of gold is hidden somewhere in a ghost town inhabited only by the mother of the four outlaws, presumed dead, who stole the treasure, and their widows. Kehoe woos each of the women in turn, attempting to wheedle out of them the whereabouts of the gold.

Comments: A waste of the Cinemascope process, this is little more than a vehicle for Clark Gable to demonstrate his devious seductive techniques and charms.

The Sheriff of Fractured Jaw (1958)

Written by: Arthur Dales

Plot: An English firearms salesman, Jonathan Tibbs (Kenneth More), is appointed sheriff of a Texas frontier town, after winning a poker game with its mayor. Surprisingly successful, he imposes his sense of gentlemanly good manners and taste on the unruly town and even manages to stop a range war.

Comments: A rather quirky parody of the western genre, with an odd mixture of American stalwarts and established British comic actors. Much of the comedy derives from the juxtaposition of Kenneth More's particular brand of English nonchalance and the townspeople's uncouthness. Jayne Mansfield plays a barroom singer, whose voice was dubbed by Connie Francis. Reputed to be the first western filmed in Spain.

A Distant Trumpet (1964)

Written by: Albert Beich, Richard Fielder and John Twist

Plot: Lieutenant Matt Hazard (Troy Donahue) is posted to Fort Delivery in the Arizona Territory. He finds himself falling in love with the wife of his commanding officer, Kitty Mainwaring (Suzanne Pleshette). When the officer is killed, Hazard seems closer to his goal, but then his own fiancée arrives. Conflict ensues with the local Indians, and Hazard finds that his sense of military duty is at odds with his sympathy for them.

Comments: Worth seeing for the epic scale of the battle scenes alone, filmed in New Mexico and Arizona. Some more intimate scenes have been cut from most copies in circulation.

WILLIAM A WELLMAN

b. 1896 d. 1975.

As a young man Wellman enjoyed a fast and furious lifestyle. He eventually also had some success as a professional ice-hockey player and was admired at one game by an actor of the silent cinema, Douglas Fairbanks, who tried to persuade him to become a film actor. When he was 19, he joined the air wing of the French Foreign Legion, but maintained his friendship with Fairbanks, and after the end of World War One, the star helped him get jobs as a film actor. Not really enjoying acting, Wellman eventually landed various jobs on the production side of the business, making his debut as director in 1920 with a western, *The Twins of Suffering Creek*. He subsequently made a string of 'B' westerns, many starring Buck Jones, and ended up at the company that was to become Paramount, where he made the flying epic *Wings* (1927), for which his talents and experience were highly suited. It was the first film to win an Academy Award as Best Picture. *The Public Enemy* (1931) is considered to be one of his masterpieces, a classic gangster film that made James Cagney into a superstar. Another all-time great is *A Star is Born* (1937). One of his most outstanding westerns is undoubtedly *The Ox-Bow Incident* (1943).

The Call of the Wild (1935)

B&W.
Written by: Gene Fowler and Leonard Praskins

Plot: Jack Thornton (Clark Gable) is a gambler who wants to get to the Alaskan gold fields. He buys Buck, a huge St. Bernard sled dog, to accompany him. Together with a companion, Shorty Hoolihan (Jack Oakie), he rescues Claire Blake (Loretta Young), whose husband has lost his way.

Comments: There is little of the original novel by Jack London left in this adaptation. Memorable for the smouldering love scenes between Clark Gable and Loretta Young, the lovable big St. Bernard, dramatic backdrops with the mountains of Washington State doubling for the Rockies, and some fine supporting performances, particularly from Jack Oakie as the sidekick and Reginald Owen as a villain.

The Robin Hood of El Dorado (1936)

B&W.
Written by: William Wellman, Joseph Calleia and Melvin Levy

Plot: The story of the real-life figure of Joaquin Murrieta (Warner Baxter), a Mexican farmer who is beaten and thrown off his land in California after his wife is killed by four Americans. He gathers a gang of like-minded rebels and sets out to terrorise the settlers, killing more than 300 people over a three-year period. Finally he is hunted down, and killed by his wife's grave.

Comments: One of the earliest western films to depict an outlaw in a sympathetic light. While it romanticises Murrieta to some extent, it also deals with the unpleasant truths about him. The real Joaquin Murrieta became a national hero in Mexico for fighting against the American oppressors. After California had been ceded to the United States the influx of Americans hungry for land and gold made life impossible for the Mexican inhabitants of the area.

The Great Man's Lady (1942)

B&W.
Written by: WL River

Plot: A 109-year-old woman, Hannah Sempler (Barbara Stanwyck), tells a biographer about her life and relationship with Ethan Hoyt (Joel McCrea), the pioneer who founded Hoyt City. In a series of flashbacks she tells how she eloped with Hoyt, suffered the hardships of frontier life with him and helped him to become successful. Through a number of misunderstandings Hoyt comes to believe that Hannah is dead and remarries. He eventually becomes a senator, and Hannah decides not to destroy his career by reappearing in his life. She lives in obscurity, until she reveals the truth in old age.

Comments: The theme of self-sacrifice was timely when the film was released in 1942 during World War Two. Barbara Stanwyck and Joel McCrea were a popular on-screen couple with the public, and appeared together in six films.

The Ox-Bow Incident (1943)

B&W.
Written by: Lamar Trotti

Plot: Gil Carter (Henry Fonda) and friend Art Croft (Harry Morgan) arrive in a frontier town in Nevada just as a posse is about to set out to find three men thought to be responsible for cattle rustling and the murder of a rancher. The posse finds three men setting up camp for the night. Despite only circumstantial evidence, they decide that they are guilty and plan to hang them. Only seven men including Gil and Art try to protest against this decision. Claiming their innocence, the three are still hanged. When the posse meets up with the sheriff it is revealed that the farmer did not die from his wounds and the three suspects were found in another town.

Comments: Based on the well-known novel of the same name by Walter Van Tilburg Clark, this is a sombre film, powerful in its uncompromising treatment of serious moral issues and disturbing psychological insight. Henry Fonda provides a beautifully controlled performance as the embodiment of moral conscience. (See also Chapter 6)

Buffalo Bill (1944)

Written by: Cecile Cramer, Aeneas MacKenzie, Clements Ripley

Plot: The film traces the life of the famous Buffalo Bill Cody (Joel McCrea) from his days as a cavalry scout to his success as a showman. He is shown in his later years protesting strongly against the treatment of the Indians. Along the way we encounter the journalist who writes books about him (Thomas Mitchell) and the women in his life: the Indian schoolteacher who loves him (Linda Darnell) and the senator's daughter (Maureen O'Hara) who becomes his wife.

Comments: While the film takes liberties with history, it evokes sympathy for the plight of the Indians, which was rare in the period.

Yellow Sky (1948)

B&W.
Written by: Lamar Trotti

Plot: A gang of outlaws robs a bank in Arizona and escapes to a ghost town, where they find an old man and his daughter. The old man has a hoard of gold. Some of the men, led by Dude (Richard Widmark), plan to cheat the old man of his gold. The leader, nicknamed Stretch (Gregory Peck), develops some affection for the daughter, which leads to his inevitable confrontation with Dude.

Comments: Based on the novel by WR Burnett, it won the WGA Screen Award for the Best Written Western Film of that year. There are many haunting views of the desert landscapes in California and Death Valley. Gregory Peck convincingly portrays the change from hardened criminal to a more sensitive human being.

Across the Wide Missouri (1951)

Written by: Talbot Jennings

Plot: In the early nineteenth century a trapper, Flint Mitchell (Clark Gable), is hunting with companions and falls in love with and weds a beautiful Blackhawk Indian princess (Maria Elena Marqués), who dies tragically.

Comments: Clearly sympathetic to the Indians, with Indian dialogue spoken in the native tongue and interpreted into English, most of the Indian roles, bar a few, were played by white or Hispanic actors. Shot in Colorado, including magnificent panorama shots of the Rocky Mountains, the haunting music contains echoes of the folk song 'Shenandoah'.

Westward the Women (1952)

B&W.
Written by: Charles Schnee

Plot: A trail boss, Buck Wyatt (Robert Taylor), is hired in 1851 by a Californian landowner Roy Whitman (John McIntire) to take a large group of women from Chicago to California to wed men they have not yet met. The women endure all kinds of trials on the way, such as inclement weather, Indian attacks and the unwelcome advances of men on the wagon train. Prominent among the women are an independently minded widow Rose Meyers (Beverly Dennis), and former showgirls Fifi Danon (Denise Darcel) and Laurie Smith (Julie Bishop).

Comments: Unusual at its time for its focus on the role of women in the opening up of the West, it depicts their trials and tribulations with unflinching realism. The screenplay was based on a story by the respected director Frank Capra.

Track of the Cat (1954)

Written by: Al Bezzerides

Plot: The members of a family that run a mountain farm are always at loggerheads with one another. When the eldest son is killed by a panther, his two younger brothers set out to kill the animal. A sub-plot revolves around whether or not one brother should marry a neighbour's daughter.

Comments: A heavy melodrama, starring Robert Mitchum and Teresa Wright, with the most powerful performance provided by Beulah Bondi as the mother. Based on a novel by Walter Van Tilburg Clark, and co-produced by John Wayne, most of the film was shot on the bleak, snow-covered Mount Rainier, and, though colour, appears virtually monochrome. It was not popular at the box office.

WILLIAM WYLER

b. 1902 d. 1981.

Born in Alsace to a Swiss father and a German mother. With family connections in the film industry, Wyler was offered a job by his mother's first cousin, Carl Laemmle, then head of Universal Studios, and he emigrated to the USA in 1920. He was given his first opportunity to direct in 1925 with the short western *Crook Buster*. For about five years he directed a large number of silent 'B' westerns. His first full-length and sound movie was the western *Hell's Heroes* (1930), and by the mid-1930s he managed to establish himself as a major director. His first big success was *Dodsworth* (1936), an adaptation of the Sinclair Lewis work about the collapse of a marriage. Other well-known Wyler films of the period are *Wuthering Heights* (1939) and *Mrs Miniver* (1942). The first western to gain him recognition in the genre was *The Westerner* (1940). During the war he made the memorable documentary *The Memphis: A Story of a Flying Fortress* (1944). Notable among his post-war films are *The Heiress* (1949), *Roman Holiday* (1953) and *Ben-Hur* (1959). His last western was *The Big Country* (1958). He made a large number of 'B' westerns (34), but most of these early films have been given scant attention by critics.

Hell's Heroes (1930)

B&W.
Written by: C Gardner Sullivan and Tom Reed

Plot: After robbing a bank, three of the outlaws (Charles Bickford, Raymond Hatton and Fred Kohler) escape into a desert. They lose their way and their horses, and come across a dying woman who is about to give birth. They agree to take the child to its father, unaware that he is one of the men they have killed in the robbery.

Comments: Unusual and moving, the film follows its source novel, *The Three Godfathers* by Peter B Kyne, very closely. Shot in the Panamint Valley and the Mojave Desert, there are no beautiful landscape shots, and the film retains a grim realism throughout, never romanticising the outlaws. It was a big success on its first release, and is still compelling today.

The Storm (1930)

B&W.
Written by: Charles Logue and John Huston

Plot: Two close friends, Burr (William 'Stage' Boyd) and Dave (Paul

Cavanagh), turn against each other when a woman arrives in their isolated cabin in the middle of a blizzard.

Comments: A well-acted, convincing film despite its rather clichéd, melodramatic plot, which, interestingly, John Huston co-wrote. The actor William 'Stage' Boyd should not be confused with the more famous film actor William Boyd (hence the nickname 'Stage').

The Westerner (1940)

B&W.
Written by: Niven Busch and Jo Swerling

Plot: Cole Hardin (Gary Cooper) is falsely accused of stealing a horse and brought before a court set up in a saloon by Judge Roy Bean (Walter Brennan). Cole discovers that the judge has a weakness for the performer Lillie Langtry (Lilian Bond), and the judge agrees to let him go free in return for obtaining a lock of Lillie's hair. Cole manages to escape from the judge and sets off for California. On the way he stops at a farm where the daughter, Jane-Ellen (Doris Davenport), persuades him that he should help the homesteaders in their fight against the cattlemen. When Cole returns to the town in the course of helping the farmers, the judge once again attempts to arrest him, but Cole gives him a lock of Jane-Ellen's hair, pretending it is Lillie's. Soon after, the judge's men set fire to the farmers' homes and crops, and Jane-Ellen's father is killed. The film culminates in a shoot-out between Cole and the judge in a theatre where Lillie is performing.

Comments: While Gary Cooper is excellent in the role of Cole, it is Walter Brennan who has won deserved critical acclaim for his performance as unprincipled villain Judge Roy Bean. Gregg Toland was responsible for the superb black-and-white cinematography. He had also worked with Wyler on *Wuthering Heights* (1939).

Friendly Persuasion (1956)

B&W.
Written by: Michael Wilson

Plot: In Indiana, in 1862, the Confederate army starts burning down towns near the home of some Quakers, who are pacifists. The father, Jess Birdwell (Gary Cooper), and his wife Eliza (Dorothy McGuire) have problems of conscience, but their son Josh (Anthony Perkins) decides to fight to defend their lives and property.

Comments: Provides many interesting insights into the Quaker way of life, with some warm comic moments. There is an interesting story behind the fact that no credits appear on the film for the screenplay, though Michael Wilson was nominated for an Oscar®. Having been summoned before the House Un-American Activities Committee in 1951, he refused to appear, pleading the Fifth Amendment, and the Academy board ruled that an Oscar® could not be awarded to anyone who refused to appear before a committee of Congress.

The Big Country (1958)

Written by: James R Webb, Sy Bartlett and Robert Wilder

Plot: An eastern sea captain, James Mckay (Gregory Peck), travels to the west to marry Patricia Terrill (Carroll Baker), but finds himself involved in a range war. Her father, Henry (Charles Bickford), is fighting with Rufus Hannassey (Burl Ives) over water rights on land belonging to Julie Maragon (Jean Simmons), and the film culminates in a shoot-out between the two embittered old men.

Comments: Burl Ives' performance won him an Oscar® as Best Supporting Actor and a Golden Globe. Memorable for its stirring musical score by Jerome Moross and the magnificence of the landscapes.

FRED ZINNEMANN

b. 1907. d. 1997.

Born in Vienna, in what was then the Austro-Hungarian Empire, for a long time Zinnemann wanted to become a violinist, but while at the University of Vienna he decided to study law. He became more and more interested in film, and became involved in the industry in Germany. Together with other German film experts he directed a semi-documentary film, a landmark in German cinema history, *People on Sunday* (*Menschen am Sonntag*), in 1930, in black and white and silent. It tells of four strangers, two men and two women, enjoying a lazy Sunday afternoon by a lake in Berlin, and is now painfully nostalgic with the knowledge of what was to come. Working with Zinnemann on the film were such later luminaries as Curt and Robert Siodmak, Edgar G Ulmer and Billy Wilder. Zinnemann finally went to America to study film, and always maintained that he was happy making films that appealed to the masses, not just as a vehicle for his own ideas. He is famously reported as saying that the three most important things about a film are 'the script, the script, the script'. He only made two westerns, but one of them, *High Noon* (1952), became a classic of the genre, and the other one of its few musicals, *Oklahoma!* (1955). Amongst other film classics, he directed *From Here to Eternity* (1953), *The Old man and the Sea* (1958), *A Man for All Seasons* (1966) and *The Day of the Jackal* (1973).

High Noon (1952)

B&W.
Written by: Carl Foreman

Plot: Former marshal Will Kane (Gary Cooper) has just married a young Quaker woman, Amy (Grace Kelly), in the small town of Hadleyville, and they are about to leave and start a new life running a general store.

News comes that a man, Frank Miller (Ian MacDonald), whom Kane had sent to prison five years before, has been released and is coming to take his revenge. Kane feels he must stay and face the man. Miller is due to arrive on the noon train, and waiting for him at the station are three of his old gang: James Pierce (Robert J Wilke), Ben Miller (Sheb Wooley) and Jack Colby (Lee Van Cleef). Kane tries to persuade the townspeople to support him but they refuse and finally he has to face the gunmen alone. Only his wife is prepared to overcome her religious scruples to support him.

Comments: Quickly recognised as a classic of the genre, *High Noon* was nominated for seven Oscars®, and won three (best actor, song and editing). It maintains a powerful sense of suspense throughout, due to skilful editing including the multiple use of telling close-ups on Gary Cooper's face. The song (composed by Dimitri Tiomkin and Ned Washington, and sung by Tex Ritter, himself a popular hero of western films) adds to the tension of the film and became a bestseller when it was re-recorded by the popular singer Frankie Laine. Some have criticised the film for depicting a community uniform in its cowardice, claiming that historically most communities always supported their lawmen, but the central figure's isolation is undoubtedly what heightens the drama. (See also Chapter 6)

Oklahoma! (1955)

Written by: Sonya Levien and William Ludwig

Plot: Set in the early 1900s when the Oklahoma Territory was about to become a state, the story focuses on the love life of a couple – Curly McLain (Gordon MacRae) and Laurey Williams (Shirley Jones) – both of whom have problems admitting their love to each other. A hired hand, Judd (Rod Steiger), is lonely and tries to come between Curly and Laurey. Another strand of the plot follows the problems of Ado Annie Carnes (Gloria Grahame) who cannot choose between the two men in her life.

Comments: A western of sorts, with many of the conventional ingredients present: cowmen, farmers and ranch hands, and the realistic, historical setting. There's much tumbling and leaping in the dance numbers, well choreographed by Agnes de Mille, but not much conflict between goodies and baddies, and it is all wrapped up in those delightful evergreen songs, by Richard Rodgers and Oscar Hammerstein, such as 'Oh What a Beautiful Mornin'', 'I Can't Say No' and 'The Surrey with the Fringe on Top'. One song by Judd, expressing his loneliness and resentment ('Lonely Room'), was omitted from the film, perhaps because it struck too dark a tone. Influential in the development of the musical, it's interesting to note that Fred Zinnemann made two westerns that were poles apart yet both equally successful in their utterly different ways.

REVALUATIONS:
SOME CLASSIC WESTERNS RECONSIDERED

This chapter brings together some critical reflections and reconsiderations of a select number of films, which have come to be regarded as truly great westerns of the so-called 'Golden Age' of the western, as outlined in chapter 5. In the present chapter only the title, date and director are cited. Further details concerning credits, cast, plot summary and a few comments can be found, and cross-referenced, under the director's name in chapter 5, and in chronological order of production.

The Ox-Bow Incident (1943)

Director: William A Wellman

Aside from interpolated sequences of rides through dusty landscapes, it becomes obvious early on that the majority of the film was made on studio sets and lots, serving to underline and reinforce the theatricality of the drama. Much of the action could be played on two stage sets: the saloon, and the encampment of the three suspected murderers at the Ox-Bow. Theatricality is also emphasised by the style of the music, the intense emotional drama of which is more conventionally associated with a thriller or murder mystery, the grandiosely evocative music of a western entirely absent.

The atmosphere of the town is an important factor in understanding the subsequent behaviour of the majority of its male inhabitants. The very first words of the film establish that the quality of the life there drives the men to seek distraction in drink, gambling and eventually vengeance. As they dismount from their horses, Gil Carter (Henry Fonda) says to his friend Art Croft (Harry Morgan), 'Deader than a Paiute's grave' (the Paiute being a local Indian tribe). The only actual sign of life in the town is the dog that wanders slowly across their path. There follows a sequence of extremely well-written dialogue, taut and full of useful information, set in the saloon, in which the concerns and interests of several of the main protagonists are established. The inaccessibility of women is alluded to, a theme which runs through the film, secondary to the central question of the nature of justice. A crudely painted picture of a voluptuous woman on the wall behind the bar reveals her curvaceous figure to the viewer, and a rather plain-looking man looks longingly at her through a curtain behind. Noticing that Gil and Art are looking at the picture, the barman points out that the man in the picture is always hoping but never gets there. To this Gil replies, 'I got a feeling she could do better'. It becomes obvious that Gil and Art are regular visitors, as they clearly know everybody by name, and Art had been expecting to find a woman called Rose Mapen there, who the barman informs him has been driven out of town by the wives. This suggests that she was a loose woman, free with her favours, and not solely devoted to Gil. Now that she is gone, such pleasure has become inaccessible to the men of the town. They depend on drink to make life bearable, as illustrated by the nice touch of showing the town drunk moving about the bar finishing others' drinks as they leave.

The focus then shifts to the issue of what to do about the murder of a local cattleman, Larry Kinkaid. Most of the men are for seeking out the rustlers and lynching them immediately, and a dispute follows between the deputy sheriff (as the sheriff is away) and the majority of the local men led by Farnley (Marc Lawrence), and the only man (apart from Gil and Art) concerned about working within the law, the storekeeper Davies (Harry Davenport). Problems arise due to matters of legal protocol. The deputy is not allowed to deputise, and the local judge cannot take over the sheriff's duty. Various individuals are vocal in their assertions that hanging is good enough for rustlers, and the majority clearly agree. A report comes in from the Mexican Pancho that three men have been seen with cattle bearing the Kinkaid brand and all set off in pursuit. Gil and Art decide that they should go with them. They are headed by a local dignitary, Major Tetley (Frank Conroy), and his sensitive, unaggressive son Gerald (William Eythe). According to Gil, Major Tetley may wear a Confederate uniform but it is doubtful whether he really fought in the Civil War.

The central part of the film consists of the long sequence during which the three men found by the posse are interrogated and the night vigil before the hanging which takes place at dawn. One of the three, Martin (Dana Andrews), claims that they are innocent. The old man is feeble-minded and the young Mexican, Juan (Anthony Quinn), who at first refuses to speak, is recognised for having a criminal record, and thus suspected of killing Kinkaid. Yet there is no incontrovertible proof that they undertook the rustling and the murder, only circumstantial evidence: they are in possession of some of Kinkaid's cattle, which Martin claims they bought off him (though someone says that Kinkaid never sells cattle after the spring round-up); there is no bill of sale; and Juan has Kinkaid's gun, which he says he found by the roadside. Some attempt is made to reach a democratic decision on whether to hang them, but it is a forgone conclusion. Only seven men vote in favour of taking the men back to face the law, and the hangings take place.

Lip service is paid to Christian morality via the Christian Sparks (Leigh Whipper), who appears to be a half-breed, and is treated, albeit affectionately, as something of an outsider, when he announces openly that he is opposed to the whole lynching process. He agrees to come along only because he believes that prayers should be said, and he sings some Christian songs and comforts the three men individually, especially the weak-minded old man. As the posse ride slowly off after the hangings his voice can be heard singing 'You got to ask the Lord forgiveness, You got to ask him for yourself', a hint that these men must now live with what they have done for the rest of their lives.

Both the absence and the presence of female elements in the film are telling. There is one scene that sits oddly in the scheme of the whole film, and takes place while the posse is riding out on their search. A stagecoach appears and the driver, thinking they are being attacked, shoots to defend himself. In the confusion Art is wounded. The stage stops, all is clarified, and out of the stage steps Rose Mapen (Mary Beth Hughes), in the company of her husband from San Francisco and his sister. All the men recognise her and there is clearly some special recognition between Rose and Gil. Her husband, perceiving this, makes Gil welcome to call on them but reminds him that she is now his wife. Then they board the stage again and set off. So why bother to include this scene at all? Apart from the picture in the bar, it is the only presentation of a 'desirable' female body in the film, now even more inaccessible. Another woman is present throughout – 'Ma' Jenny Grier (Jane Darwell) – but she is far from any man's ideal, and behaves much more like a fellow man in her manner and general attitudes. Throughout the interrogation scene she is heard cackling frequently off screen, visible only a few times; and what she is laughing at we never know, but it sounds like a mockery of the entire proceedings.

The other 'feminine' element in the film is manifest in Gerald Tetley, the son of Major Tetley, through an insult directed at him by his father who refers to him as a 'female boy'. His father thinks he's weak, cowardly and unmanly; representative of the sensitive human qualities usually associated with a woman from the perspective of an aggressive male attempting to prove his dominance and judgement. If this film were remade in the twenty-first century Gerald might be presented more openly as homosexual, but in 1943 the qualities which are deemed acceptable in a woman are despised by the authoritarian father. Tetley orders his son to take part in whipping the horses from under the accused when they are hung. Gerald refuses and his father says: 'I'll have no female boys bearing my name. You'll do your part, and say no more.' After they all return to the town in the knowledge that Kinkaid is still alive and the three rustlers have been captured elsewhere, Tetley locks his son out of their house. Gerald finally stands up to his father and shouts through the door, 'Does it make you feel that there may be some weakness in you that other men might discover and whisper about?' Major Tetley goes through an inner door and we hear the sound of a gunshot; presumably he has shot himself.

When Gil finally reads out Martin's letter to his wife, in a stage whisper, so that all the other men lined up against the bar can hear, it becomes clear that Martin had a sure sense of what constitutes true justice ('It's the very conscience of humanity'). The film ends on a note that confirms any true family values were absent from the lives of most of the townsmen. Art asks, 'Where're we going?' and Gil replies, as if there's only one option, 'He wanted his wife to get this letter, didn't he? He said there was nobody to look after the kids, didn't he?' And as they ride out the way they came in, the town seems deader than it ever was, and the same dog crosses back across the street.

High Noon (1952)

Director: Fred Zinnemann

Fred Zinnemann's *High Noon* is a masterly piece of filmmaking. It is rare indeed that screenplay, acting, shot composition, editing and music complement each other so well, yet seem so fluid. While the dialogue is stark, it is at all times essential, and there is scarcely a line spoken that doesn't resonate with the motifs of the film. Its visual aspects are so eloquent that one is scarcely aware that there are sequences containing little or no dialogue; they have the force of montage in the silent cinema at its most accomplished (in the films of Eisenstein and Murnau for instance). The theme song, performed by Tex Ritter, accompanies several such sequences, and they would otherwise be silent, devoid even of sound effects.

Most films in the 1950s started with a separate title sequence, which was followed by introductory scenes. Nowadays, the viewer is accustomed to long (often seemingly interminable) sequences prior to the titles. Zinnemann opted to combine the titles with an introductory sequence from the moment the first image appears on the screen, so that the viewer dare not let attention lapse throughout the film, for fear of missing a detail. As the titles and main credits appear a man is sitting on a rock on a hill, and another approaches him on horseback. They meet and exchange words. A third man arrives, and all set off to a nearby town, causing consternation to everyone who sees them. Accompanying this action is a song, already relating to the main elements of the story in summary, which, like a traditional ballad, evokes associations of a legend being retold. Still, after the titles, there is no dialogue. The first sound effect is that of the church bell tolling. People stare and hurry off to tell others. A woman crosses herself.

The coincidence of three circumstances is clearly significant: it is Sunday morning, Marshal Will Kane (Gary Cooper) is marrying the Quaker Amy Fowler Kane (Grace Kelly), and news is coming via the telegraph of the imminent arrival of a released killer, Frank Miller (Ian MacDonald), on the noon train. The scene is set for the conflict of multifarious values and loyalties, all within a condensed timespan. The countdown to noon is more than just an effective suspense device: it defines the dramatic structure of the film. Events unfold in almost real time. The climax is preset; only the outcome is uncertain.

The film accords in fact with Aristotle's description of classical tragedy in combining the three unities of time, place and action. The difference, of course, is that the tragedy is averted. The manner in which it is averted criticises the values and double standards of the community of Hadleyville. Kane's decision to face Frank Miller in an inevitable gunfight challenges the limits of the bourgeois morality that he has been instrumental in enabling in the community. What the community owe him is made clear in a speech by Mayor Jonas Henderson (Thomas Mitchell) during the meeting in the church. Kane turns to larger groups to garner support, the drinkers in the saloon and the people in the church. In the saloon he is met by stony silence and fear, and the sympathies of many of the men present lie with Miller. Nervous, mocking laughter follows Kane as he leaves the saloon, having failed in his attempt. He enters the church in the middle of a sermon, and the priest is at first hostile, in part because Kane had not been a regular churchgoer. He relents when Kane reveals his wife is a Quaker, and initially he finds sympathy and enthusiasm. Gradually, however, opinions turn against him, and Henderson delivers the final rejection: it would be better for all concerned if he left town while there is still time.

This draws a connection with a significant sequence near the beginning of the film, after Kane is married in the church, when the news of Frank Miller's imminent arrival first reaches him. Kane's first reaction is to agree to flee. He and his wife hurry out of town on a buggy, but then he has a change of heart. Frank Miller has vowed to kill him, and fleeing will only postpone, not prevent, the confrontation.

His decision to brave it out challenges the limits of friendship too. His old friend, the previous marshal, Martin Howe (Lon Chaney Jr.), sees no reason why he should finish his days lying in a dusty street. The only people who will commit themselves to Kane unreservedly are either naïve or ignorant of the true danger of the situation. The old drunk, Jimmy (William Newell), blind in one eye, is willing, but only to prove that he is still man enough. Young Johnny (Ralph Reed), 14 years old but pretending to be 16, will stand by him, but only out of childish idealism, and Kane will not risk the boy's life. Johnny is the only person whom Kane looks on with affection before he and his wife ride out of town at the end of the film. Deputy sheriff Herb (James Millican) commits himself from the start and takes a deputy's badge, but he had assumed that many others would follow his example and join them. When finally it is obvious that there will only be he and Kane, he begs to be freed from his promise for the sake of his wife and children.

Two women of dissimilar natures feature prominently in the film: Amy and Mrs Ramirez (Katy Jurado). Amy is a devoted wife but an idealistic one. Her Quaker beliefs will not allow her to contemplate condoning her husband's decision. By her own account, she saw her own father and brother killed by guns, which contributed to her decision to become a Quaker, and now she faces having a husband die in the same way. Helen Ramirez is a somewhat ambiguous figure. She is Mexican, with her voluptuousness deliberately emphasised, and the owner of the saloon. It is never made explicit but she is undoubtedly a woman of looser morals, or easy virtue, compared with Amy. Having had a relationship at one time with Frank Miller, she is referred to as a friend of Kane's. How intimate that friendship may have become is never revealed but in one telling sequence the clerk in the hotel makes a comment to Kane as he goes up the stairs to Helen's room, which suggests he already knows where it is: 'Think you can find it alright?' Kane hesitates, seems about to remonstrate, but is aware of Amy's presence and goes on. At the end of a conversation with Helen, they exchange remarks in Spanish. These are not translated in the film, but are suggestive of their former intimacy (Helen: 'One year without seeing you.' Kane: 'I know.'). The two women differ also in their final resolution. They ride to the station together and board the train. A little later shots are heard from the town. Helen stays on the train, having sold her property and concerned for her personal safety, but Amy hurries off and runs back into the town. It is she who single-handedly averts a tragic outcome. Kane kills two of the men, and two remain, including Frank Miller. When the other man is reloading his gun, he is shot. As he falls forward, Amy is revealed at the window of the sheriff's office with a gun in her hand. Not only has she overcome her Quaker principles, she has shot a man in the back. Kane is now free to confront and kill Miller. There is one final twist when Miller takes Amy as a hostage, but Amy fights back and distracts Miller sufficiently for Kane to shoot him. Before riding out of the town together, Kane discards his sheriff's badge without even a second glance. Everything it stood for has been undermined by the self-interest of the townsfolk.

Cinematographically, the film contains several noteworthy sequences: when the judge decides to leave there is a montage of images culminating in a shot of the empty chair in which Frank Miller sat when he uttered the threat of revenge on Kane. This image recurs near the end of the film. At the strike of noon there is another impressive montage of close-ups of all the people whom Kane has approached, including the two women. There is also one deceptively simple shot of Kane standing alone in the main street: the camera backs away and rises steadily high above the town, showing his complete isolation. Finally, in the overall structure of the film, there are the constant reminders of the passing of time, with shots of clocks in various locations. The events appear to be running in real time, but some take much longer than the clocks would seem to indicate. As Alfred Hitchcock famously did in the fairground climax of *Strangers on a Train* one year before in 1951, Zinnemann stretched time, a device which intensified the sense of suspense.

Shane (1953)

Director: George Stevens

Viewing *Shane* again, 54 years after it was first released, it has lost nothing of its force and consistency of vision. The pace is firm and steady, never too slow nor too hurried. No single shot or scene is super-fluous to the furtherance of its themes.

The question often arises whether a film has dated or not, usually with respect to characters' interpersonal behaviour, the presentation of sexual relations, the depiction of violence and conventions of acting. While *Shane* is identifiably of its era, the 1950s, there is a frank truthful-ness and realism contained within its conventions. Both violence and love are restrained and more powerful for it. This restraint is a central coordinating principle in the film, one embodied in its central figure – the mysterious gunman, who has learned that killing a man leaves a shadow over the soul for life, the eponymous hero Shane.

Shane enters the valley as he leaves it, literally, for the penultimate shot of the film echoes the first: at the beginning he rides into frame from the left down into the valley, and at the end he rides out of the valley again and out of frame to the left. What has happened in his life before his time in the valley and what will happen after remain a mystery; we only know that once in the past he killed a man. He is welcomed on his arrival at their farm by Joe Starrett, his wife Marian and son Joey. It is Joey who first sees Shane approach and throughout the film many aspects of Shane are presented through the boy's eyes. At the beginning, the boy is pretending to stalk a stag watering nearby. Into view, behind the animal, rides Shane, and Joey transfers his awe from the animal to the mysterious stranger, whom he quickly begins to idolise. When some of the cattle-owner Ryker's men arrive to harass Starrett into leaving his land, Starrett believes for a while that Shane is in league with them. Shane, the stranger, at first remains aloof, but when the bullying tactics of Ryker's men become apparent and Shane is asked to identify himself, he replies, 'I'm a friend of Starrett's'.

Shane is encouraged by the family to stay and is offered work as a farmhand, but at all times he is more than that: he complements the world of each member of the family. Starrett has the moral strength and determination to do battle with Ryker, but he is also a loving husband and father, and must at all times think of the safety of his family; Shane is the outsider with no ties but a firm sense of right and the coolheaded self-control to carry his actions through. The strength of the two men together is symbolised in the scene in which only together can they chop down and topple over an old tree trunk, which had been in an inconvenient position close to the house. Marian is clearly attracted by the strength she perceives in Shane, of a good man gone astray. The boy Joey is the most outspoken in his love and admiration for Shane with all the innocence of a child, yet such confessions are always indi-rect and handled with supreme subtlety. Even when Joey finally tells his mother, 'I love Shane', we overhear it through the closed door of his bedroom.

The treatment of the relationship between Shane and Marian is one of the most accomplished features of the film. The truth is in the nuances. In one scene Shane suddenly leaves the room at the end of a meal, and no explanation is given. In another, Starrett asks his wife, 'What's the matter, Marian?' She replies, 'Nothing'. And this too is never explained. The viewer is left to deduce a connection between these two unexplained events. Marian comes closest to expressing her feelings in two specific sequences. One occurs when Shane has gone out in the rain to sleep in the barn. She looks at him and speaks to him with great gentleness through the window. The other occurs late in the film when Shane is about to set off into town and she is concerned for his safety. Her look and hesitation speak volumes. In both sequences, Joey is also present in the background, and both are viewed from behind Shane, over his shoulder, as though from his perspective. Shane can never forget, even in their most intimate moments, that Marian is a mother. Marian's growing awareness of the strength of her own feelings is made clear when, after seeing Shane out the door, she turns to her husband and says, 'Hold me', before they enter their bedroom together, feeling the need perhaps to be protected from herself.

It's through these sequences that one of the prime concerns of all the settlers, as well as of the Starrett family and Shane, is emphasised: the maintenance of the family and family values. This provides the dominant conflict in the film. On the one hand, there's Ryker and his gang, who claim that the open range is theirs to run their cattle wherever they will, and who virtually live in the general store, spending their free time in drinking. Then there are the settlers, struggling to establish a firm foothold for their families in the remote land. When Ryker's men burn down the homestead of Lewis and his wife, as they are about to leave, tired of the endless harassment, it is Shane who reminds them all that their concern for their families should come first. The outsider, the non-family man, perceives most acutely what they are in danger of forgetting. In a wilderness, a family is the only real source of security, particularly with the remoteness of any other source of moral authority, a fact that is emphasised on several occasions. One of Ryker's men reminds us that there is no law and order 'within a 100-mile ride', and later someone echoes, 'The law is a three-day ride from here'. The owner of the general store is the only man who is accorded a vaguely defined sense of authority by even Ryker and his gang, presumably because his control of the supply of goods enables him to exert some power over their lives. The remote location of both the township and the settlers' houses is frequently emphasised by long shots of the few meagre log-buildings on the endless plains, with the towering cold majesty of the mountains beyond.

The film clearly invites the viewer to consider the situation of the Starrett family as a microcosm of the whole of America at the time. The 10th wedding anniversary of Starrett and his wife coincides with Independence Day. At the dance in celebration of both events, Starrett relates the two in his speech, indicating that the freedom they had all won was the freedom to live as they wanted and where they wanted, stressing that he had chosen freely to marry his wife on that day, further emphasis of how central the commitment to family life is to the survival of the settlers. It is a strength of the film, however, that the conflict between Ryker and Starrett is never simply black and white. In the final confrontation between the two men, Ryker is allowed to plead his case with some conviction: he feels that he and his like freed up the plains for the settlers. Starrett reminds him that they do not owe everything to him for it was the pioneers who originally cleared the way. If Ryker has ever possessed a free-spirited individualism he has lost it over his obsession to retain control of the land he claims to have freed. The character of Calloway is an interesting bridge between the Ryker gang and the home-steaders. He is shown in a few shots looking uneasy on the occasion of the funeral of Torrey, the southerner, who was provoked by the hired gunman Wilson, so that he could shoot him. It is Calloway who informs Shane that when Starrett goes into town to meet Ryker, he will find the cards 'stacked against him'.

There are several allusions in the film to the lingering resentment between southerners and northerners after the Civil War. Initially, this is manifest in the form of innocent jokes made at Torrey's expense, with one settler playing the southern song 'Dixie' mockingly on the mouth organ. But later Wilson takes advantage of this sensitivity in his provocation of Torrey, and Shane taunts Wilson with an insult to Yankees in their final confrontation.

The character of Wilson is brilliantly conceived as a direct contrast to Shane. He has few lines but his presence dominates every scene he is in. While Wilson is a man without conscience, Shane is its embodiment, but both men share the qualities of coolness and restraint. This is shown vividly in the sequence when they meet at Starrett's farm, eyeing each other unflinchingly. Wilson is like a panther waiting to strike, the only unequivocally evil person in the film. His stance, mode of dress and even walk foreshadow the cold-blooded killers of the 'spaghetti western', which still lay decades in the future.

There are many other themes that can be fruitfully pursued in the film, for instance the significance of the absence of institutions, such as a church or a school. The settlers create their own sense of religious community by singing hymns on important occasions, with 'Abide with Me' being the all-purpose hymn for Independence Day and funerals, when the more learned member present is asked to say prayers. And when Starrett is pleading with Lewis not to leave, he promises that they will build not only a church but a school for their children, a sign that this community has not been fully civilised. There is also the role of the music in the film (by Victor Young), which does more than just echo the mood of each scene, it comments on it, in gentle satirical references to the 'Dixie' theme for example, hinting at imminent danger, and suggesting the feelings of love that are expressed with such careful restraint throughout the film.

The Man From Laramie (1955)

Director: Anthony Mann

In many ways the film tells a simple story, but in a compelling manner. The background and motivation of the man who prefers to describe himself simply as being from Laramie, Will Lockhart (James Stewart), is revealed only gradually, as it pleases him. He prefers to remain anonymous as long as possible. There are certainly surprising turns in the plot but not sudden twists. It is possible to narrow down the options for the identity of the man he is seeking long before the end of the film. The main fascination of the film is with the six central characters and how they interact, with a significant extra seventh, Will's loyal companion Charley (Wallace Ford), who serves to provide useful information at specific junctures. Because the central characters and their interrelations are complex, it is not possible to predict how any particular situation will resolve itself. Even young Dave (Alex Nicol), the tearaway loose cannon of the Waggoman family, is unpredictable, if only because of his childishness. One senses that he will bring about some disaster through a restless act, but it is not clear beforehand what form it will take.

The central relationships are established quite early in the film. Lockhart delivers three wagons of supplies, with a small group of helpers, to the Waggoman mercantile store in Coronado, an isolated town in an area surrounded by Apache Indians. He befriends the young woman who runs the store, Barbara (Cathy O'Donnell), who turns out to be a relative of the landowning family, the Waggomans. On her advice he decides to gather salt from the nearby salt flats, which she assures him is common land, to serve as a load for his return journey. While his men are loading the salt a group of men headed by Dave Waggoman arrive, claiming that they are digging on Waggoman land. Dave and his men proceed to tip the wagons over and set fire to them. Vic Hansbro (Arthur Kennedy), who also works as foreman for the Waggomans, arrives and breaks up the attack, apologising to Lockhart. Subsequently

Lockhart fights with Dave, when he sees him in the middle of the town, and this time ends up fighting with Vic too in a rough-and-tumble among the cattle pens. A mature and tough-looking woman (who later proves to be a Miss Canady, played by Aline MacMahon) intervenes to stop Dave storming in to help Vic. Finally Dave's father, the main landowner in the area, Alec Waggoman (Donald Crisp), arrives, and puts a stop to the squabble, with a promise to pay Lockhart the next day for the damage caused to his wagons. Miss Canady takes Lockhart off to her ranch hoping to persuade him to work for her. Vic proves to be the man Barbara has promised herself to in marriage. With that the central characters and their relationships are established.

Barbara wants to leave the town and start a new life, but Vic feels tied to the Waggoman family, as the old man trusts him like a son and has given him a verbal promise to leave him a share in his property. It has become clear, however, that the old man's main interest is to ensure that someone will take care of his son, whose irresponsibility he is perfectly aware of. It is also revealed that Dave resents this treatment by his father and being bossed around by Vic. Barbara and Lockhart are in the meantime clearly becoming attracted to each other, though neither makes a move. Alec Waggoman is portrayed as hard and determined but fair in his dealings. There is love in him and the need for love, but his success has depended on neatly classifying people and controlling them. At his first meeting with Lockhart he asks him: 'We keep out dirt farmers and fence raisers. Which are you?' Lockhart replies: 'I'm from Laramie'. A significant improvement on his previous, vague statement to Barbara: 'I belong where I am'. Both remarks indicate that he regards himself primarily as a free individual, not one to be pinned down to any particular role or identity. The neighbour, Miss Canady, has a long-standing feud with Alec Waggoman, which is one of the reasons why she wants to employ Lockhart, who, she feels, will stand up to the old man. Later in the film we learn that when she was young she had been engaged to him. His blindness (incipient for much of the film but made complete by a fall) makes him aware finally of how dependent he is on others, and brings him and Miss Canady close together again.

Somewhere in this web of relationships are the clues to the identity of the man Lockhart is looking for and the reason why he seeks him. Only very gradually are the answers to both mysteries provided. In the occasional meetings with Charley, who acts as scout for Lockhart, we learn more about his background and his motives: someone dear to him has been killed in an Apache raid using repeating rifles, and he is determined to find out who has been supplying them to the Indians. We also learn that he has been a military man, and occasionally in conversation with others, such as Miss Canady, he lets slip some reference to army life. It is only to the two women, Barbara and Miss Canady, that he reveals, separately, details of his motivation: his young brother, still very much a kid, was killed in one such Apache raid. Only when Vic is seen trying to prevent Dave signaling to the Apaches to arrange a handover of the hidden hoard of repeating rifles does it become clear that Vic has been party to the project. Vic, it appears, might be the man Lockhart is looking for.

There is something stark and elemental in the central conflicts of *The Man From Laramie*: sons, whether blood or adoptive, competing for a father's love; revenge meted out Old Testament-style, if not exactly an eye for an eye, then certainly a hand for a hand, when Dave shoots Lockhart in his gun hand after Lockhart has wounded his. There is evidence of a more civilised morality in the minds of some of the characters, but it faces the intractable lifestyle of the West where law barely holds sway. The town sheriff is well intentioned but lacks any real power. He takes Lockhart's gun away when he is suspected of murdering the dubious Boldt (Jack Elam) and puts him in jail, but Alec Waggoman's influence soon gets him out again. Old Waggoman tries to temper his rage with fairness, but when his son is killed and it is assumed that Lockhart is the culprit, he rides out with the intention of killing him but gives up when he stumbles from his horse onto the ground. Lockhart, when vengeance is within his grasp, lets Vic go. The

Apache apparently do not share this more civilised conscience. For them Vic has simply gone back on their deal and destroyed the guns. He is shot by the repeating rifles he has doubtless provided them with. Unnecessarily, but symbolically, one of them shoots an arrow into his body.

With fine, subtle editing, the film's cinematography is always effective and never showy. Particularly memorable is the long take of Lockhart walking towards the camera across the large square of the town and turning off only at the last minute to right of camera to hit out at Dave. The shot draws out audience expectation that something dramatic will happen, though what exactly is kept uncertain until the penultimate moment. The same can be said of the entire film.

The Searchers (1956)

Director: John Ford

The impression that remains most vividly long after a viewing of John Ford's *The Searchers* is the deep, fiery orange-red of the landscape, the gaunt, haunting, desolate and intimidating landscape of Monument Valley, that Ford returned to again and again as the setting for many of his finest westerns. Throughout the film, however far Ethan (John Wayne) and Martin (Jeffrey Hunter) travel in search of Lucy and Debbie, both kidnapped by Comanches after the slaughter of their family, and however many years they are away, they never seem to escape that lifeless, soulless landscape. The homestead of Ethan's brother exists in a wilderness, and the township of their neighbours likewise. A visit by anyone is an event of major significance and calls for coffee and whatever delicacies are available. This isolation is the key to the relationship between Martin and Laurie Jorgensen (Vera Miles), who have known each other since childhood, so that Martin has never considered it necessary to express his love openly. When Martin is away for years on end, this isolation explains how Laurie can consider marrying the hapless Charlie (Ken Curtis). What other options has she?

It is the isolation also which makes the family so vulnerable to Indian attack. Only the two young girls can escape alive, kidnapped by the marauding Indians. This sets in motion the endless-seeming search, the driving force of the film, by Ethan and Martin. Ethan is driven by the desire for revenge, Martin by sibling love. There are many questions which are left deliberately unanswered in the film. It is known from Ethan's own report that the Civil War finished three years previously, but it is never made clear what he has been doing since, nor why he suddenly decided to seek out his brother and family. This discretion is a quality which lends the film its strength and subtlety, and is a far cry from the explicit violence of latter-day westerns. The worst of the violence happens off screen, hinted at but not described. When it is revealed that the attack on a neighbour's cattle was only a ruse by the Comanche to distract the settlers away from their homes, and Ethan and Martin return to find his brother's homestead razed to the ground, Ethan prevents Martin from seeing the carnage inside the house. Nor is the audience allowed even a glimpse. After they have been travelling for some time, Ethan, Martin and Brad (who had been courting Lucy) realise that a small group of Indians has separated from the others and gone off through a small canyon. Arranging to meet the others on the other side, Ethan goes to investigate. When he returns to the others he is taciturn, full of suppressed anger. To Martin's query he admits only that he has probably lost his blanket. Later he is forced to reveal to both men that he found Lucy's body in the canyon and buried it as best he could wrapped in his blanket. Again we are left to imagine the condition that the body is in. Brad, in anger, rides off to seek revenge. We hear shots and must assume the worst. Ethan maintains his discretion not only in matters of violence but also relating to sex. Later he speculates on Debbie's fate if she has been allowed to survive and grow up among the Comanches. He explains to Martin: 'They'll keep her till she's an age to…' and the rest is left to the imagination.

Ethan's hatred of the Indians appears to be long standing. The murder of his only close family was seemingly the last straw. Nor is his hatred born of ignorance, for he reveals frequently in the film a profound knowledge of the ways of the Indians and their thought processes. In the first part of the film this brings him into conflict with the Reverend, also known as Captain Johnston Clayton (Ward Bond), who is the only moral authority in the settlement. Ethan is as stubborn as they come, set in them, and convinced that there will never be any need for him to modify them. He has a catchphrase which he reiterates several times in the film, whenever it is suggested that he might think otherwise: 'That'll be the day!' It is this single-minded commitment that all but brings about a tragic ending to the story. When he discovers that Debbie has adopted Comanche ways he at first determines to kill her. Uncertainty about what he will in fact do is maintained right up till he has chased her to a cave and held her up high with his arms. He might still dash her against the rocks, but instead says comfortingly, 'Let's go home, Debbie'.

The way in which the Indians are presented in the film is its one questionable aspect, though it undoubtedly reflects the attitudes of the majority of white Americans in the historical period in which the film is set: they are talked of only as savages bent on massacre. There are very few indications of their humanity. Ethan justifies his preference for killing Debbie with the words, 'Living with Comanches ain't being alive'. Only the warrior Scar is allowed to answer in any way which truly challenges the white man's assumed superiority. When Ethan and Scar first meet, Ethan comes right up close to him, face to face, and finally admits reluctantly, 'You speak good American. Someone teach you?' As Scar takes him into his tepee Scar retaliates, 'You speak good Comanche. Someone teach you?' When the Reverend and his men raid the Comanche camp, the order is given to disperse the horses and we see some general disarray in the camp, with only a quick glimpse of a man or woman running with a child to safety. What follows is left to the imagination. The film focuses on Ethan's pursuit of Debbie, after which it cuts to a scene of comic relief as the Reverend has a wound in his backside attended to. Are we to assume that the Reverend's men merely dispersed the

Indians and did not wreak any more violent revenge? Is the editing here discreet or does it idealise?

Comic relief is, as in most of Ford's films, very much in evidence, often in surprising juxtaposition with the tragic. It verges on caricature and farce with the old Mr Jorgensen and the simple-minded Mose, and especially in the spoiled wedding ceremony and subsequent fight between Martin and Charlie. The love affair between Martin and Laurie is also presented as a childish game, and it could be argued that their childishness is the result of the isolation from any more extensive society during their upbringing, yet both behave with frequent displays of petulance and peevishness, more suitable in ten-year-olds than adults. Martin is part Indian, and Ethan assumes that his childishness derives from the less civilised aspect of his personality: 'That's the Indian in you.'

The stronger, more mature love in the film is clearly perceived to be that within the family, between siblings, and between parents and children. Most human emotions are clearly unrefined and not yet fully civilised. Both the people and the country are still in their infancy. As Mrs Jorgensen says, 'Some day this country's going to be a fine place to be'. But not yet.

The final image of the film is of Ethan walking away from the house, viewed through the doorway, as it closes, after everybody else has come inside. He remains an outsider and will not live to see that fine country of which Mrs Jorgensen dreams. It is true that in him love overcame the desire for vengeance in the end, but it seems unlikely that he will ever really change ('That'll be the day!').

3.10 To Yuma (1957)

Director: Delmer Daves

Comparisons are often justly drawn between *3.10 To Yuma* and Fred Zinnemann's *High Noon* (1952), released only a few years previously, the likelihood being that the success of the latter influenced the former. The similarities are obvious: suspense focused on the arrival of a train, conflict between two men, one acting out of moral concerns and the other clearly not, the dwindling support of the townsfolk, the support of a loyal wife, and, not least, superb black-and-white photography. But *3.10 To Yuma* also explores other issues and aspects of character.

At the centre of the film is the relationship between Dan Evans (Van Heflin) and Bill Wade (Glenn Ford), how they become involved in each other's lives, and how from polar opposite positions in terms of moral conscience, they form a remarkable bond, which enables them to save each other's life. From the beginning Wade is depicted as an outlaw of complex sensitivity: he can kill brutally out of self-interest then grow concerned about the disposal of the victim's body. Having drawn Evans' cattle into the path of a stagecoach to facilitate holding it up, he mercilessly kills one of his own men, when the stage guard uses him as a hostage, and then immediately kills the guard. Shortly after, he is advising the owner of the stage line how best to ensure that the guard's body is returned to his family. Evans, meanwhile, watches all this, powerless to act in the presence of his own sons, because of his concern for their safety. Other gestures reveal Wade's dual nature, and make the final outcome of the film credible. He tells his henchman to reassure Evans that he will get his cattle back, and promises to leave the horses they have commandeered outside the town so that they can be reclaimed. From the start Wade is depicted, in Ford's memorable performance, as a canny and perceptive judge of character. There are frequent shots of him eyeing the behaviour of others thoughtfully, and he takes in all that he hears about Evans' family background and financial straits. Despite his insight into others, and ability to influence and control them, he also has a weakness which makes him act unwisely on occasion, endangering his own safety: he likes attractive and submissive women, preferably barroom singers. Having fooled the sheriff and his hastily assembled posse concerning the circumstances of the attack on the stagecoach, he delays his own escape while his men disperse, because of his attraction to the barmaid. This gives the sheriff time to discover the truth from the survivors of the attack, return and capture him.

There is a complicated ruse at the heart of the film which provides the motive for plot development: the sheriff plans to deceive Wade's men by arranging for a faked accident with the stage that is carrying Wade to jail. While the stagecoach is being righted, a switch is made, and Wade stays at Evans' home until he and other deputies can take him to the town of Contention to wait there for the 3.10. train to Yuma the next day. Thus Wade comes into close contact with Evans' family and attempts to work his charms on his wife.

Evans has only agreed to take on the job as deputy, at a payment of $200, out of desperation when he cannot obtain a loan to tide him over a period of drought. Witness to the discussion about the possibility of a loan while he was being held in handcuffs in the saloon, Wade makes use of all this knowledge during the climactic confrontation between the two men, which takes place in the stuffy, claustrophobic confines of a hotel room in Contention, while they await the arrival of the 3.10 train. He taunts and provokes Evans, tempting him with money beyond his dreams, until the moment when Evans wavers and is on the verge of accepting. He also reminds Evans how hard life is for his wife, and how she must have been really beautiful before she met him.

Throughout almost the whole film a sardonic smile lurks around Wade's lips: he looks, it seems, from a superior vantage point on the absurdities of the behaviour of others. He knows the selfishness and essential cowardliness of human nature, and predicts accurately that the other deputies will flee in fear and that even the determined Butterfield, the owner of the stage line, will desert him in the end. When Butterfield reassures him, 'I'll walk with you every step of the way to the station', Wade responds, 'We'll see. We'll see.'

Then a change comes over Wade, which by necessity is barely perceptible, so that the outcome of the film remains uncertain till the end. It is only in retrospect that the significance of a particular scene can be understood. Evans' wife has followed him in a buggy and risks her own life in coming into the hotel, where she sees the town drunk Alex (Henry Jones) hanging from the chandelier. Coming into the room, in front of Wade but with eyes only for her husband, she pours out her feelings to him. She does not mince the difficulties and the hardship, 'all the worry, all the work, all the hurts of life', and is willing to put up with it all just for them to be together. Significantly she says she does not want pearls. which is precisely what Wade had promised the barmaid on leaving her earlier. Whatever may happen she will stay by him. Intercut are shots of Wade watching. There is something visibly different about his smile, which at this stage is ambiguous. At the end of the film it becomes clear, when he voluntarily jumps onto the luggage car of the train to Yuma as it passes them, to the amazement of Evans. Evans asks him why he did it and he says it was because he saved his life back in the hotel when the son of the stage guard had tried to kill him. It is now clear, however, that Wade had been impressed by the strength of the bond of love between Evans and his wife, which enables them to overcome all hardship.

Evans has also developed greater firmness and clarity in terms of his own moral conscience. As he explains to his wife, Alex, the town drunk, had sacrificed himself for justice: 'Do you think I can do less?' In the course of events he has also learned something about his captive, so that at the end he is able to trust Wade to do what he says he will do. As they stand by the train which is gathering speed, he asks Wade, 'How do I know you will jump?' Wade replies, 'You'll have to trust me on this one'.

OTHER GEMS

There are a number of westerns from its 'Golden Age' which are well worth attention but not by the directors most closely associated with the genre, as listed in Chapter 5. In some cases they are by well-known directors who have only occasionally turned their hand to westerns or by not-so-well-known directors who have managed to make some good and original films in the genre. There are also those unusual productions of arguable quality, which have nevertheless gained some fame or notoriety. For whatever reason it would be a pity to neglect them. They are listed here in chronological order.

The Plainsman (1936)

B&W.
Director: Cecil B DeMille
Written by: Harold Lamb, Jeanie MacPherson, Lynn Riggs and Waldemar Young

Plot: In the period after the Civil War John Lattimer (Charles Bickford) is planning to sell rifles to the Indians. Wild Bill Hickok (Gary Cooper) learns that Indians have attacked an army garrison and reports the fact to General George Custer (John Miljan) who sends in Buffalo Bill (James Ellison) with a wagon-train of arms to the rescue. Hickok is sent to conduct talks with the Cheyenne, but has to help Calamity Jane (Jean Arthur) out of a bit of trouble with Indians. They are both captured and taken to the Indian camp. The film ends with Hickok killing Lattimer but being shot in the back during a card game.

Comments: A well-made and entertaining film which plays fast and loose with historical accuracy, introducing many famed heroes and one heroine of the West and inventing myriad encounters between them. Abraham Lincoln even gets a look in but is called away urgently by his wife, who reminds him that they will be late for the theatre.

Western Union (1941)

Director: Fritz Lang
Written by: Robert Carson

Plot: In the 1860s Vance Shaw (Randolph Scott), a former outlaw, helps the chief engineer of Western Union, Edward Creighton (Dean Jagger), to set up the telegraph line between Omaha, Nebraska and Salt Lake City, Utah. His main job is to defend the enterprise from Indians and others. A former friend, Jack Slade (Barton MacLane), who is still an outlaw, attempts to foil their plans.

Comments: An impressive handling of the genre by respected director Fritz Lang. A compelling pace and plenty of action involving Indian raids, outlaw attacks and a forest fire hold the attention. Lang made two other westerns, *The Return of Frank James* (1940), which was a moody affair with little action, and *Rancho Notorious* (1952), an unconventional western about a hideout for outlaws run by a former saloon singer (Marlene Dietrich). More conventional than each, *Western Union* is no less accomplished for that.

Annie Get Your Gun (1950)

Director: George Sidney
Written by: Sidney Sheldon

Plot: The film tells the story of Annie Oakley (Betty Hutton), a historical person famed for her sharpshooting. She falls in love with but also comes into conflict with the star sharpshooter, Frank Butler (Howard Keel), in Buffalo Bill's Wild West Show.

Comments: Based on the original Broadway musical by Dorothy Fields, Herbert Fields and Irving Berlin. Before the show actually got to the screen there were endless problems with finding suitable main performers, and several changes in director. Originally Busby Berkeley was going to direct, then Charles Walters, but finally George Sidney was chosen. The producers of the original show, Richard Rodgers and Oscar Hammerstein, had wanted Jerome Kern to do the musical score, but finally agreed on Irving Berlin. The film was a great success both at the box office and with the critics. It has more hit songs than almost any other Hollywood musical, including 'The Girl That I Marry', 'Doin' What Comes Naturally', 'Anything You Can Do', 'I've Got the Sun In the Morning', 'You Can't Get a Man With a Gun' and the all-time rousing finale song 'There's No Business Like Show Business'.

Red Mountain (1951)

Director: William Dieterle
Written by: John Meredyth Lucas

Plot: During the Civil War a Confederate officer, Brett Sherwood (Alan Ladd), joins John Quantrell (John Ireland) and his rebel cavalry unit to try and prevent a Union victory. On the way Sherwood tries to find an assayer who had stolen his land claim before the war. When the assayer is found dead, the townsfolk accuse an ex-Confederate soldier Lane Waldron (Arthur Kennedy). Sherwood rescues him from a hanging but Waldron now tries to put the blame for the murder onto him. The situation is further complicated by the fact that Sherwood and Waldron's fiancée Chris (Lizabeth Scott) are attracted to each other.

Comments: Well-acted and constructed, the character of Quantrell was based loosely on the historical figure of William Clark Quantrill, with the spelling of the name changed so that the studio could deny the film's relation to reality.

Broken Lance (1954)

Director: Edward Dmytryk
Written by: Richard Murphy

Plot: A rancher, Matt Devereaux (Spencer Tracy), has a second wife who is a Comanche Indian (Katy Jurado). He organises a raid on a copper smelting works, which is polluting his water. For this his youngest son, Joe (Robert Wagner), shoulders the responsibility and goes to prison. When he comes out of prison, his father is dead, his mother has gone back to her people, and his three half-brothers by his father's first wife have taken his inheritance.

Comments: The film has excellently written dialogue and deals with many sensitive issues, including those of filial and sibling conflict, and attitudes to people of mixed race. It helped establish Robert Wagner as an actor in leading roles.

Johnny Guitar (1954)

Director: Nicholas Ray
Written by: Philip Yordan

Plot: Vienna (Joan Crawford), the proud woman owner of a classy gambling saloon in a remote part of Arizona, plans to build a whole new town to take advantage of the fact that the railroad will be coming through near her saloon, and she will become rich. But she has reckoned without the opposition of Emma Small (Mercedes McCambridge), a leader of the local community. Vienna is supported by a former lover, Johnny Guitar (Sterling Hayden), who is more than he seems.

Comments: The film has stirred up much intellectual debate and acquired cult status in France. Its complex and ambiguous sexuality has made it accessible to various schools of cultural criticism. Does it present a Marxist view of the West, or is it a lesbian inversion of the conventional western traditions? Two central male roles are a dancer and a guitar player, while the main female role, Vienna, has most of the attributes of the conventional male gang leader with her black clothes, six-shooters and decision-making. Action is also generated by the two women. More concerned to explore neuroses from a modern psychological perspective than reflect anything resembling the historical West, the film features powerful performances and excellent dialogue to stimulate jaded palates.

The Sheepman (1958)

Director: George Marshall
Written by: William Bowers and James Edward Grant

Plot: A sheep farmer, Jason Sweet (Glenn Ford), arrives in a cattle town and clearly intends to graze his sheep on the range, to the consternation of the local cattle farmers. The townsfolk, under the corrupt leadership of Colonel Stephen Bedford (Leslie Nielsen), plan to run him out of town.

Comments: Not a very widely shown film, it has much to recommend it: a well-controlled performance by Glenn Ford with subtle touches of irony, and a hilarious turn by Mickey Shaughnessy as the would-be tough man who is constantly outwitted by Sweet.

Warlock (1959)

Director: Edward Dmytryk
Written by: Robert Alan Arthur

Plot: Warlock is a lawless town and run by a cruel gang. A group of its inhabitants hire Clay Blaisdell (Henry Fonda), a frontier marshal, to sort out their problems. Blaisdell, however, is not above a little corruption himself, and expects he will be granted several privileges. He is accompanied by a club-footed gambling friend, Tom Morgan (Anthony Quinn). The townsfolk begin to feel that they should get rid of the new marshal, and turn to the deputy, Johnny Gannon (Richard Widmark), himself a former outlaw. The situation is complicated by the fact that Gannon is developing a relationship with Lily Dollar (Dorothy Malone), a former lover of Morgan's, who accuses Blaisdell and Morgan of having murdered her fiancé.

Comments: A rather convoluted film, there is much focus on the psychological make-up of the central characters, with a hint of homosexual hero-worship in that of Tom Morgan, unusual in a film of this era. Henry Fonda gives a masterly performance as a man at odds with his present self and his past.

The Alamo (1960)

Director: John Wayne
Written by: James Edward Grant

Plot: Texas was the most northern province of Mexico in 1836 and its inhabitants were rebelling against the rule of General Santa Anna (Ruben Padilla). When General Sam Houston (Richard Boone) has difficulty raising an army against Santa Anna, Colonel William Travis (Laurence Harvey) helps out with his small troop. Another small group of volunteers under Colonel Jim Bowie (Richard Widmark) also comes to their aid, and there is some rivalry between the two groups. Harmony of sorts is brought about by the agency of Davy Crockett (John Wayne). All are now ready to face the enormous force of the advancing Mexican army in the ruined Spanish mission buildings known as the Alamo.

Comments: For more than 14 years John Wayne had dreamed of directing this famous true story. Though he had always wanted to direct right from the start of his career, this marked his debut at the helm. The casting of the British actor Laurence Harvey, who became known in America after his Oscar® nomination for the British film *Room at the Top* (1959), was suggested by John Ford. Wayne also cast many actors with whom he had worked in the past, notably in films directed by John Ford, and he gave a small but important role to his own son, Patrick Wayne. It is a long and ambitious film, with many fine action sequences and capable stunt work by Cliff Lyons, who was also second unit director. The film produced a hit with the theme song 'The Green Leaves of Summer'. Though not greatly praised by critics, it was a box-office success both at home and abroad.

One-Eyed Jacks (1961)

Director: Marlon Brando
Written by: Guy Trosper and Calder Willingham

Plot: Two bank robbers, Rio (Marlon Brando) and Dad Longworth (Karl Malden), are running from the law after robbing a bank in Mexico. Dad makes off with the money while leaving Rio to be caught and put in prison for five years. When Rio manages to escape he sets out to find Dad and take his revenge. He finds Dad as a law-abiding sheriff in a small town in California, gains his trust again and then makes his step-daughter pregnant.

Comments: The film displays many signs of Brando's notorious self-indulgence. Instead of the scheduled 60 days the film took six months to complete. Endless hours were spent waiting for small details of settings to be just right. The final version that Brando produced was about five hours long, and Paramount Studios cut it down to 141 minutes, to make it commercially viable. In the original version it was ambiguous who was the villain and who the hero of the piece, if anyone. In the cut version, Rio is clearly the hero and Dad the villain. Despite the studio's efforts, it remained a financial loss but is of interest for its offbeat character and for good performances. Ben Johnson in particular, is convincing as villain Bob Amory. The title refers to the fact that in a pack of cards it is only possible to see one side of the Jack's face. Rio compares Dad to such a 'one-eyed jack', adding 'but I see the other side of your face'. This is the only film that Marlon Brando directed.

Lonely Are the Brave (1962)

B&W.
Director: David Miller
Written by: Dalton Trumbo

Plot: Set in modern-day New Mexico, the film tells of Jack Burns (Kirk Douglas), whose best friend is put in jail for helping Mexicans get across the border illegally. He gets himself jailed too so that he can help him escape, only to find that his friend does not want to take the risk. Instead he escapes himself and sets off for the Mexican border on horseback. He is pursued by a posse fully equipped with the most up-to-date modern gadgetry, but manages to evade capture. Finally, he is hit by a truck while crossing a road, and in a last bid for freedom gets himself killed.

Comments: This thought-provoking film was not a success at the box office, but is worth seeking out. Many questions about Burns' character and motivation are left unanswered, which is part of the film's fascination. Although in a contemporary setting, it relies for its effect on knowledge of the independent loner in the tradition of the western genre.

McLintock (1963)

Director: Andrew V McLaglen
Written by: James Edward Grant

Plot: George Washington McLintock (John Wayne) is a ranch owner with a town named after him. The Comanche Indians ask him to protect their interests when they are about to be put under the control of a government agent. His estranged wife (Maureen O'Hara) arrives with the aim of getting a divorce and gaining custody of their 17-year-old daughter Becky (Stefanie Powers). After lively Fourth of July celebrations McLintock finally loses patience with his wife, chases her around the town into a mud pool and ends up spanking her.

Comments: The film provides a lively mixture of action and slapstick comedy and has remained popular with audiences. It was quite a Wayne family affair, with son Michael Wayne producing, other son Patrick Wayne as Dev Warren, one of Becky's suitors, and Aissa Wayne (aged 7) as young Alice Warren. Andrew V McLaglen was to direct three more westerns with John Wayne: *The Undefeated* (1969), *Chisum* (1970) and *Cahill, U.S. Marshal* (1973).

Shenandoah (1965)

Director: Andrew V McClaglen
Written by: James Lee Barrett

Plot: A widower, Charles Anderson (James Stewart), runs a farm in Shenandoah, Virginia, and lives with his six sons and one daughter. Though the Civil War is raging, he ignores it. The youngest son, Boy (Philip Alford), is mistaken for a Confederate and taken away by some Union soldiers. Anderson leaves his son James (Patrick Wayne) and his second wife Ann (Katharine Ross) in charge of the farm, and sets off with his daughter Jennie (Rosemary Forsyth) and his other sons to find Boy. Their search is fruitless and they decide to return home. The son Jacob (Glenn Corbett) is killed in an ambush by the rebels. And when they arrive home they discover that James and Ann have been murdered by two deserters. Only the baby survives. The following Sunday the lost son, Boy, comes into the church, injured and on crutches.

Comments: The plot reads like that of the heaviest of melodramas, but it is a mark of James Stewart's abilities as an actor that he depicts so convincingly the growing sufferings of a man whom Fate seems to have marked out for tragedy. It might sound unlikely, but the film was the basis for a successful Broadway musical, which managed to win itself a Tony award.

The Rare Breed (1966)

Director: Andrew V McLaglen
Written by: Ric Hardman

Plot: Martha Price (Maureen O'Hara) wants to fulfil her dead husband's dream of introducing Hereford cattle in the American West. Together with her daughter, Hilary (Juliet Mills), she gets the help of Sam 'Bulldog' Burnett (James Stewart) to transport a single Hereford bull called Vindicator to a Texan breeder.

Comments: Not one of McLaglen's better westerns, but James Stewart's performance is reliably decent. The story is based on historical accounts of the introduction of the Hereford breed into America.

Custer of the West (1967)

Director: Robert Siodmak
Written by: Bernard Gordon and Julian Halevy

Plot: This familiar story details the period when US Army General George Armstrong Custer was given command of the Seventh Cavalry and had to deal with warring tribes of Indians. He fought at the battle of Little Bighorn where he and his troops were completely wiped out.

Comments: In Robert Shaw's performance, Custer is neither incompetent nor brave to the point of foolhardiness, as he has sometimes been portrayed. Instead he is a man whose attitudes are out of kilter with those of the times and his circumstances. The film exhibits a particular trend towards revisionism in the depiction of famous historical figures in the period when it was made.

Hombre (1967)

Director: Martin Ritt
Written by: Irving Ravetch and Harriet Frank Jr.

Plot: John Russell (Paul Newman), also known as 'Hombre', is a white man who was raised among the Apache Indians. He is travelling on a stagecoach with an Indian agent, Dr. Alex Favor (Fredric March), and his wife Audra (Barbara Rush), a dangerous outlaw, Cicero Grimes (Richard Boone), and a woman of dubious reputation, Jessie (Diane Cilento). When they are attacked by outlaws they all have to seek safety in a mining camp. Because of his background Hombre cannot sympathise with Audra, who hates Indians, but he is forced to reconsider his priorities when her life is in danger.

Comments: The situation and moral dilemmas clearly echo John Ford's *Stagecoach*, but this film's treatment of the issues are more self-conscious. It is also much more pessimistic in its outcome.

Hang 'Em High (1968)

Director: Ted Post
Written by: Leonard Freeman and Mel Goldberg

Plot: After having bought a herd of cattle from a rancher, Jed Cooper (Clint Eastwood) is driving them across the Rio Grande when he is surrounded by a group of men who say that the original owner of the cattle has been found dead. The prime suspect, Cooper is hanged and left for dead, then saved by a passing marshal Dave Bliss (Ben Johnson). Cooper is made a deputy by a magistrate and given the authority to find the men who attempted to hang him.

Comments: Very much Eastwood's production, he cast many of the actors and arranged for Ted Post, who had directed many of the episodes for the TV series *Rawhide*, to helm. Eastwood's character in the film is reminiscent of the persona he had developed in the 'spaghetti westerns' he had made with Sergio Leone.

Butch Cassidy and the Sundance Kid (1969)

Director: George Roy Hill
Written by: William Goldman

Plot: Butch Cassidy (Paul Newman) and the Sundance Kid (Robert Redford) lead a gang of robbers. Butch is the 'brains' in the gang and Sundance is the skilled man of action. The Law tires of their escapades and a special posse is set up to pursue them. Eventually Butch suggests they escape to Bolivia, but they are pursued even there and eventually get their comeuppance.

Comments: This could be described as a 'revisionist western' but only in the loosest possible sense of the term. Revisionism usually implies a reassessment and righting of the historical account, but this film takes enormous liberties with the known facts and aims instead for romanticised adventure. Enormous fun, it's acted with great panache by the two leads, but the real Butch Cassidy was a cowboy in the 1890s who drifted into robbery to survive and the Sundance Kid was a brutal gunfighter. Their female companion, Etta Place (played by Katharine Ross in the film), was in all likelihood a prostitute. Nor were the Pinkerton detectives likely to have been the cruel killers depicted here. Nevertheless, with its witty dialogue, it makes for enjoyable viewing and features the well-known song by Burt Bacharach, 'Raindrops Keep Fallin' On My Head'.

Mackenna's Gold (1969)

Director: J Lee Thompson
Written by: Carl Foreman

Plot: Marshal Sam Mackenna (Gregory Peck) kills an old Apache in self-defence and commits to memory the details of an old map the Indian possessed which is said to reveal where the so-called 'Canyon of Gold' is situated. Mackenna is kidnapped by the Mexican leader of a band of outlaws called Colorado (Omar Sharif) who wants Mackenna to lead him to the canyon. Apache Indians are also pursuing them for vengeance. Finally it comes to a confrontation between Mackenna and Colorado atop the famed 'Canyon of Gold'.

Comments: This rather improbable adventure tale does function well as successful entertainment, and boasts an impressive cast. Very popular at the box office, it features much exciting action and a famous sensuous seduction scene at a waterhole. The screenplay was based on a novel by Will Henry.

Chisum (1970)

Director: Andrew V McLaglen
Written by: Andrew J Fenady

Plot: Cattle owner John Chisum (John Wayne) is the largest ranch owner in Lincoln County, New Mexico, also one of the founders of the town of Lincoln. Worried about the attempts of Lawrence Murphy (Forrest Tucker) to try and take over many local businesses and property by dubious means, at first he and others try to fight him within the bounds of the law, but he discovers that Murphy has the local lawmen in his pay too.

Comments: The story is based on the historical Lincoln County Cattle War. It also features famous historical figures such as Billy the Kid (Geoffrey Deuel), the man who eventually killed him, Pat Garrett (Glenn Corbett), and the Englishman who became a friend of Billy the Kid, Henry Tunstall (Patric Knowles). There is a consistently powerful performance by Ben Johnson as Pepper, Chisum's foreman who is always grumbling.

Soldier Blue (1970)

Director: Ralph Nelson
Written by: John Gay

Plot: Honus Gent (Peter Strauss), a rather naïve young soldier known as 'Soldier Blue' and Kathy Maribel Lee, known as 'Cresta' (Candice Bergen), are travelling with the troop guarding the paymaster, when they are attacked by Cheyenne. The two manage to escape the general massacre. Honus is gradually falling in love with 'Cresta' but cannot accept her critical views about the army. Finally they reach an army post. 'Cresta', who lived with the Cheyenne for two years, discovers a plan to annihilate the Indians and rides out to warn them.

Comments: The film presents a very one-sided view of historical events. In its attempt to right the balance it swings too far in the other direction. The army are presented as unprincipled and inhuman, and the Cheyenne as utterly pure and innocent. Some scenes of violence are particularly distasteful, for example when the breasts of Indian women are sliced off and tossed to and fro on the ends of sabres. The film was made at the height of the anti-war protests during the Vietnam War, and it is likely that audiences were being invited to draw comparisons unfavourable to the American army.

Chato's Land (1972)

Director: Michael Winner
Written by: Gerald Wilson

Plot: An Indian, Pardon Chato (Charles Bronson), is provoked into fighting and eventually killing a sheriff who constantly makes racist remarks to him. Captain Quincey Whitmore (Jack Palance) organises a posse to track him down. The posse becomes obsessed with vengeance, killing Chato's son and raping his wife, leaving her naked in the desert. Chato manages to save his wife and then starts to pursue each member of the posse, killing them one by one.

Comments: One of the good qualities of this film is its attempt to explore the motives of each member of the posse in some depth, and it leans heavily in favour of the plight of the Indians. So well did Winner and Bronson work together that they went on to collaborate on five more films.

Jeremiah Johnson (1972)

Director: Sydney Pollack
Written by: John Milius and Edward Anhalt

Plot: The film tells the story of Jeremiah Johnson (Robert Redford) who seeks spiritual peace away from civilisation in the heart of the Rocky Mountains, but is persecuted by Indians and eventually has to fight one of their warriors. He also becomes acquainted with a strange Indian woman (Allyn Ann McLerie) and an old trapper known as Bear Claw Chris Lapp (Will Geer).

Comments: The screenplay was based on the biography of an historical figure entitled 'Crow Killer' by Raymond W Thorp and a novel called 'Mountain Man' by Vardis Fisher. While there is much to praise in the film, in particular its beautiful cinematography and uplifting philosophy of life, it is also rather meandering with no clear goal or conclusion.

Cahill (1973)

Director: Andrew V McLaglen
Written by: Harry Julian Fink and Rita M Fink

Plot: US Marshal JD Cahill (John Wayne) returns home to Valentine, Texas, after taking part in a manhunt, to find that the bank has been robbed, the sheriff and deputy murdered, and his two young teenage sons persuaded by an outlaw, Abe Fraser (George Kennedy), to take part in a bank robbery. Feeling neglected by their father they thought it was the best way to gain his attention.

Comments: Not the best of John Wayne films, but fascinating for its unusual plot, which gave the star a chance to combine his tough no-nonsense persona with that of a concerned, loving father.

COMIC WESTERNS

From the earliest days of cinema, comedy has flourished across every genre, and all the major comics of silent films made their slapstick versions of the western idiom: Chaplin, Keaton and even Douglas Fairbanks who often introduced some comic interludes into his films, as in the western *The Man from Painted Post* (1917), directed by Joseph Henabery. Though many such films may not have had historical western settings, they utilised the myths and character types. Charlie Chaplin's *The Gold Rush* (1926) tells of the experiences of a lone prospector, the Tramp, going to the Klondike in search of gold, and features a confrontation with the notorious outlaw Black Larsen (Tom Murray). Buster Keaton's *The General* (1927) is set firmly in the historical period of the Civil War, even if the storyline is unconventional for a western. It tells of a train driver, Johnnie Gray, who loves two things in life: his train, 'The General', and a certain Miss Annabelle Lee. At the beginning of the Civil War he is not allowed to become an ordinary soldier because he is more valuable as an engine-driver. Unfortunately, Annabelle does not believe him and regards him as a coward. But when spies from the Union army capture the train while Annabelle is aboard, Johnny has to prove himself a true hero. There is much gentle comedy in *Cowboy from Brooklyn* (1938), directed by Lloyd Bacon, which is set in the contemporary world, but pokes fun at the traditional image of the cowboy. Elly Jordan (Dick Powell) is an actor who wants to get a job at a radio station as a crooning cowboy, but must prove he is the genuine article. The year after this, one of the most memorable comic westerns of its time appeared,

Destry Rides Again (1939), was directed by George Marshall.

Some westerns included in other chapters of this book are comedies or contain strong comic elements. The following summaries and comments on individual films are in chronological order.

Destry Rides Again (1939)

B&W.
Director: George Marshall
Written by: Felix Jackson, Henry Myers and Gertrude Purcell

Plot: A naïve pacifist sheriff, Tom Destry (James Stewart), arrives in a rough town on a stagecoach. He is persuaded to take on the job of marshal to help clean the town up, but begins to be distracted by a saloon bar singer called Frenchy (Marlene Dietrich).

Comments: From the opening sequence the conventional image of the tough lawman is undermined. When he arrives on a stagecoach Destry is unarmed and carrying a parasol and a canary. He promptly goes into the Last Chance Saloon and orders a glass of milk. There had already been another straight adaptation in 1932 of the novel by Max Brand, with the same title as George Marshall's version. This earlier version was later known as *Justice Rides Again* to avoid confusion, directed by Ben Stoloff, and starring Tom Mix. There was to be yet another straight version in 1954, directed again by George Marshall and starring Audie Murphy. None of the versions stayed close to the plot of the novel, and it has been the 1939 film, with Stewart and Dietrich, that has acquired cult status. It has many memorable scenes, notably the barroom brawl between Frenchy and Lily Belle (Una Merkel). The music is also delightful, and includes a classic Dietrich rendering of 'See What the Boys in the Backroom Will Have'. The film has the rare (even unique perhaps) distinction of having become famous for a line which does not feature in the final cut due to the censors. When Marlene Dietrich stuffs some money down her cleavage, she said in the uncut version, 'There's gold in them thar' hills'.

The Paleface (1948)

Director: Norman Z McLeod
Written by: Edmund Hartman and Frank Tashlin

Plot: Calamity Jane (Jane Russell) is released from prison to help find a gang of outlaws who are running guns to the Indians. To create a cover story for herself she seduces and marries an incompetent and cowardly dentist, 'Painless' Peter Potter (Bob Hope). Their wagon train is attacked and Jane's skill with the gun saves them, but she gives the credit to Potter, who thereby becomes a hero but also a target for both the Indians and the gunrunners.

Comments: The film still works as a great comedy, with many classic Hope one-liners ('Brave men run in my family', 'It's not the Indians I'm afraid of. It's their attitudes'). It also includes the song which was to become a big hit for Dinah Shore: 'Buttons and Bows' (by Ray Evans and Jay Livingston).

Heller in Pink Tights (1960)

Director: George Cukor
Written by: Walter Bernstein and Dudley Nichols

Plot: A theatrical troupe travels around the remote western regions, hotly pursued by debtors and Indians.

Comments: Angela Rossini (Sophia Loren in a blond wig) is an actress who is constantly getting herself into trouble. The famous star of the silent cinema, Ramon Novarro, appears in his last film role playing a villainous banker with great style. It is all harmless fun but there's little genuine wit. The film was based on the novel 'Heller with a Gun' by Louis L'Amour.

Cat Ballou (1965)

Director: Elliot Silverstein
Written by: Walter Newman and Frank Pierson

Plot: The film is set in the 1890s. When the father of Catherine 'Cat' Ballou (Jane Fonda) is killed, she decides to hire a famous gunfighter, Kid Shelleen (Lee Marvin), but discovers that her knowledge of the West is out of date, for over the last 20 years Shelleen has become a drunk.

Comments: Lee Marvin turned in one of his most memorable performances in this film and won an Oscar® as Best Actor. He also won awards at other festivals around the world for this performance. In fact he plays two roles in the film, also taking the part of his own evil brother, Tim Strawn. A memorable feature of the film is the frequent appearance at unexpected moments of Stubby Kaye and Nat 'King' Cole, as singing narrators who move the story along with their western-style ballads.

Carry On Cowboy (1965)

Director: Gerald Thomas
Written by: Talbot Rothwell

Plot: The town of Stodge City is controlled by the Rumpo Kid (Sid James) and his gang. The local judge sends for a new marshal to sort the problems out. When a sanitary inspector arrives he is mistaken for the new marshal. Eventually he manages to get rid of the Rumpo Kid in an ingenious way by using his expert knowledge of drains.

Comments: The film has all the elements one has come to expect from 'Carry On' films: crude sexual and lavatorial innuendo, camp performances and slapstick comedy, from the stalwarts of the series Sid James, Kenneth Williams, Jim Dale, and so on. There is an amusing send-up of Gary Cooper's lone walk down the street in *High Noon*, and Charles Hawtrey is hilarious as Chief Big Heap.

Support Your Local Sheriff (1969)

Director: Burt Kennedy
Written by: William Bowers

Plot: Jason McCullough (James Garner) is a cowboy on his way to Australia who takes on the job of sheriff in a small gold town. He arrests a young killer (Bruce Dern), which angers his father, Pa Danby (Walter Brennan), and his brothers.

Comments: One of the more subtly worked out parodies of the genre, which avoids the tendency to simply string a lot of jokes together as some of the later comic westerns tended to. There is exaggeration without tastelessness or self-indulgence (as in the case of *Blazing Saddles*). Jack Elam, who had long played serious roles in westerns to great acclaim, here reveals a notable talent for comedy in the role of McCullough's deputy Jake.

Paint Your Wagon (1969)

Director: Joshua Logan
Written by: Paddy Chayefsky and Alan J Lerner

Plot: The story is set in the period of the gold rush in California, and concerns two prospectors, Ben Rumson (Lee Marvin) and Pardner (Clint Eastwood), who become partners and agree to share everything, including a wife, Elizabeth (Jean Seberg). The town, No Name, is a lawless den of vice and gambling. Pardner and Elizabeth become increasingly attracted to each other to the exclusion of Ben, whom Elizabeth nevertheless does not want to give up.

Comments: The film is not strictly speaking a comedy or parody, but based on the hit Broadway musical by Lerner and Loewe, with the same title, from 1951. It is, however, full of comic interludes, and the triangular relationship between Ben, Pardner and Elizabeth was not part of the original musical. The film may not be the most successful screen adaptation of a musical, but it's visually very pleasing and features many enjoyable songs, which became hits in their own right, including the unlikely renditions of 'Wandrin' Star' by Lee Marvin and 'I Talk to the Trees' by Clint Eastwood.

My Name Is Nobody (Mio nome è Nessuno) (1973)

Director: Tonino Valerii
Written by: Ernesto Gastaldi

Plot: In 1899 a young gunman, Nobody (Terence Hill), idolises an older gunfighter, Jack Beauregard (Henry Fonda), and wants to compete with him, but Beauregard just wants to give it all up, retire and sail off to Europe.

Comments: This is a difficult film to classify. While there are strong arguments in favour of describing it as a 'spaghetti western', it lacks the ethos and bleak vision of humanity in those films. It was, however, developed from an idea by the master of the 'spaghetti western', Sergio Leone, and directed by one of his protégés. Most of the actors too are Italian. The musical score, by Ennio Morricone, includes a parody of Wagner's 'The Ride of the Valkyries' and passages which are self-parodies, including allusions to his own music for earlier films directed by Sergio Leone. The film was made predominantly in America. There are various allusions to the cinematic history of the western, with a shot showing Sam Peckinpah's name on a gravestone. Beauregard is also encouraged to take on a gang of 150 men known as the 'Wild Bunch'. There are some cameo roles by veterans of the American western genre, such as RG Armstrong and Geoffrey Lewis. It might be more appropriate to describe it as a 'pasta salad' western.

Kid Blue (1973)

Director: James Frawley
Written by: Edwin Shrake

Plot: Set in Texas around 1900 the film tells of an outlaw (Dennis Hopper) who is forced to realise that he cannot survive through crime. Instead he tries to settle down in the quiet town of Dimebox, but soon gets into trouble when his friend's wife tries to seduce him.

Comments: Despite delightful moments, the film is not particularly original in its parody of the genre.

Blazing Saddles (1974)

Director: Mel Brooks
Written by: Mel Brooks, Norman Steinberg, Richard Pryor, Andrew Bergman and Alan Uger

Plot: A corrupt businessman, Hedley Lemar (Harvey Korman), terrorises a town with his gang. The sheriff is killed and Lemar persuades the state governor, William J LePetomane (Mel Brooks), to appoint a black sheriff (Cleavon Little), but the new sheriff turns against him. After that the plot becomes a device for stringing gags together.

Comments: The film makes fun of every conceivable convention of the western genre. It is full of hilarious cameo performances and absurd conceits: Gene Wilder plays the Waco Kid, an alcoholic gunman; Mel Brooks also plays an Indian who speaks Yiddish; Count Basie appears conducting a jazz band in the middle of the desert; and Madeline Kahn, as Lili Von Shtupp, does an impersonation of Marlene Dietrich, with clear allusions to the latter's performance in *Destry Rides Again* (1939). The title song, performed by the veteran of title songs Frankie Laine, is also self-parody. It has to be said that while there are many brilliantly funny jokes in the film, there is also much vulgarity and bad taste, qualities which have doubtless contributed to its huge success.

Rancho Deluxe (1975)

Director: Frank Perry
Written by: Thomas McGuane

Plot: Jack McKee (Jeff Bridges) and Cecil Colson (Sam Waterston) are two cattle rustlers in Montana who persuade a couple of ranch hands to help them steal a herd of cattle. But one of the gang becomes enamoured with the daughter of the man who has been employed to pursue them. They finally end up in a prison camp known as 'Rancho Deluxe'.

Comments: A pleasant, light comedy set in modern-day Montana, but the main ingredients of the story are firmly rooted in the conventions of the genre.

Hearts of the West (aka *Hollywood Cowboy*) (1975)

Director: Howard Zieff
Written by: Rob Thompson

Plot: In the early 1930s Lewis Tater (Jeff Bridges), a would-be writer of western stories in the mode of his hero Zane Grey, enrols for a correspondence course, but discovers that he is being cheated by confidence men. He pursues them into the desert and becomes involved with a film company making cheap westerns.

Comments: Amusing without being hilarious, the film features accomplished and enjoyable performances.

The Duchess and the Dirtwater Fox (1976)

Director: Melvin Frank
Written by: Melvin Frank, Jack Rose and Barry Sandler

Plot: Charlie Malloy, known as the 'Dirtwater Fox' (George Segal), is a crooked gambler who joins forces with a dance-hall performer, Amanda Quaid, known as 'Duchess Swansbury' (Goldie Hawn). Together they try to find some stolen money, which is hidden in the desert.

Comments: Hardly the funniest of comedies, though Goldie Hawn managed to garner a Golden Globe nomination as 'Best Motion Picture Actress in a Musical or Comedy'.

From Noon Till Three (1976)

Director: Frank D Gilroy
Written by: Frank D Gilroy

Plot: A beautiful young widow, Amanda (Jill Ireland), has an affair with a barely accomplished bank robber, Graham Dorsey (Charles Bronson). Thinking he is dead, she embroiders the truth about their relationship and makes him into a legendary hero. Her version of their affair is turned into stories, dramatised, and even becomes the theme of a popular song. Graham, however, returns, very much alive, and now nobody, not even the woman, believes he is who he claims to be: they prefer the legend.

Comments: A gentle comedy, with a nice ironic twist.

Buffalo Bill and the Indians, or Sitting Bull's History Lesson (1976)

Director: Robert Altman
Written by: Robert Altman and Alan Rudolph

Plot: The story takes place during winter performances of Buffalo Bill's famous show in the 1880s. Buffalo Bill (Paul Newman) is depicted as a charlatan who maintains a myth to keep the audience coming in. Chief Sitting Bull is portrayed as the true hero of the West.

Comments: Very loosely based on the play 'Indians' (1969) by Arthur Kopit, the humour is weak and the satire never really gains strength. Frank Kaquitts provides the most notable performance as Chief Sitting Bull. Some typical Altman qualities are in evidence: the overlapping and at times incomprehensible dialogue, the evocation of an entire world and complex interrelations of characters, all creating the impression that one has stepped back in time and is eavesdropping.

The Frisco Kid (1979)

Director: Robert Aldrich
Written by: Michael Elias and Frank Shaw

Plot: A poor orthodox rabbi called Avram Belinski (Gene Wilder) is sent to lead a Jewish community in San Francisco. His money is stolen in Philadelphia and he has to continue on foot. He has many hair-raising experiences, but eventually meets up with an outlaw with a heart of gold, Tommy Lillard (Harrison Ford).

Comments: Despite many potentially funny scenes, such as the sequence in which Indians are taught new dances, the comedy never really takes off.

Rustlers' Rhapsody (1985)

Director: Hugh Wilson
Written by: Hugh Wilson

Plot: A singing cowboy, Rex O'Herlihan (Tom Berenger), and his friend Bob Barber (Patrick Wayne) are traveling through the West and arrive at a small town where a corrupt cattle baron (Andy Griffith) is exploiting the local sheepmen. The cattle baron and a group of Italian cowboys attempt to throw O'Herlihan out of town.

Comments: The most memorable scene in the film is undoubtedly the opening sequence, in which a cinema audience is seen watching an old black-and-white western. The narrator wonders how such a film would be made nowadays, and the film within the film changes from black and white to colour as the parody begins. Andy Griffith is very amusing as a camp cattle baron, and there are strong performances by GW Bailey as the local drunk and Marilu Henner as the dance-hall girl. The Italian cowboys wear long raincoats down to their ankles, whatever the weather, in a clear send-up of the 'spaghetti western' convention.

Three Amigos (1986)

Director: John Landis
Written by: Steve Martin, Lorne Michaels and Randy Newman

Plot: Three film performers, Lucky Day (Steve Martin), Dusty Bottoms (Chevy Chase) and Ned Nederlander (Martin Short), who form a singing trio, dressed in elaborate, idealised Mexican costumes, find that their film series, apparently in the silent era, has been given the axe. They receive a job offer from Mexico, related to someone who is called El Guapo (Alfonso Arau). On arrival they discover that El Guapo is in fact a cruel leader of a gang of thugs, who terrorise a village. The hapless trio attempts to destroy the gang with the occasional reprise of song and guitar numbers from their films.

Comments: Much of the humour stems from the fact that the Three Amigos of the title are now forced to live up to the constantly smiling, indefatigably optimistic trio of idealistic crime-fighters they had created on screen, but in a world of desperate brutality and poverty. The film has many entertaining and occasional hilarious moments. The potential is there for a more perceptive satire, but, that said, it is enormous fun.

Back to the Future, Part III (1990)

Director: Robert Zemeckis
Written by: Robert Zemeckis and Bob Gale

Plot: Marty McFly (Michael J Fox) travels back to the nineteenth-century version of his hometown, Hill Valley, to rescue his friend, the bizarre time-travelling inventor, Doc Brown (Christopher Lloyd), who is trapped in the year 1885. He finds the first generation of his family that has just arrived from Ireland, and gives his name as Clint Eastwood. The Doc in the meantime has inconveniently fallen in love with schoolteacher Clara Clayton (Mary Steenburgen).

Comments: The film features many allusions to classic westerns and western actors. Famed cowboy actor Harry Carey Jr. appears in a saloon scene, and Marty resorts to his memories of the gunfight in *A Fistful of Dollars* to aid him in his own confrontation with gunfighters. In the Doc's courting of the schoolteacher there are clear allusions to the dance sequence in John Ford's *My Darling Clementine*. The film also features stunning special effects, though they are related to the futuristic elements of the story rather than the world of the western, which is the main focus of the film.

City Slickers (1991)

Director: Ron Underwood
Written by: Lowell Ganz and Babaloo Mandel

Plot: Three lifelong friends – Mitch Robbins (Billy Crystal), Phil Berquist (Daniel Stern) and Ed Furillo (Bruno Kirby) – live settled middle-class married lives in New York. Worried at the prospect of middle age, they decide to set off on a cattle drive from Mexico to Colorado. After various escapades they are helped on their way by an archetypal tough cowboy, Curly (Jack Palance).

Comments: What starts as a light comedy involving encounters with various bizarre characters, or caricatures, including a couple of black dentists and some Jewish tycoons, ends on a moral note as the three friends ga n real insight into who they are. There was a rather ineffectual sequel with many of the same cast in 1994, called *City Slickers II: Curly's Revenge*.

Maverick (1994)

Director: Richard Donner
Written by: William Goldman

Plot: Brett Maverick (Mel Gibson), a clever gambler, deft with the cards, arrives in a small town and joins a card game, in which an attractive woman, Annabelle Bransford (Jodie Foster), is taking part. The story focuses on the exploits of the group of gamblers: Maverick, Annabelle, a con man called The Commodore (James Coburn), a bad loser called Angel (Alfred Molina),who shoots people when he goes down, and an Indian Chief (Graham Greene).

Comments: The film includes much charming cinematography, incorporating classic western locations, and riverboats on wide rivers, but the humour is light and whimsical, with little real wit. James Garner, who played the character of Maverick in the original TV series and appears here as a retired lawman, Zane Cooper, proves that he can still outshine the rest of the cast with his effortless nonchalance.

THE ITALIAN CONNECTION

The term 'spaghetti western' is sometimes used to denote all westerns made outside America (including Germany and Russia) and particularly the large number of westerns made overall in Italy. Most people associate the term, however, with a specific small number of films produced by Italian directors in the 1960s and 1970s. Westerns were actually being made in Italy as early as the 1940s. Notable films of that period are *Una Signora dell'ovest* (*Woman of the West*) (1942), directed by Carl Koch, and starring Rossano Brazzi, a later luminary of Hollywood. Another such film is *Il fanciullo del West* (*Boy of the West*) (1943), directed by Giorgio Ferroni. These were made during the Fascist period in Italy, when it was not possible to import American films, and were clearly produced as substitutes to please popular taste. Two directors are closely associated with the phase of 'spaghetti westerns' in the 1960s and 1970s: Sergio Leone and Sergio Corbucci. Sergio Corbucci became most well known for two films, featuring the character of Django, which explored cold-blooded violence in ways which shocked many viewers. One other film which has come to be regarded as a 'spaghetti western' is *China 9, Liberty 37* (1978), directed by Monte Hellman. It is the story of a gunfighter saved from hanging by corrupt railroad bosses on the condition that he kill another former gunfighter, so that they can obtain his land. The film features many Italian actors, but also Warren Oates and Jenny Agutter. Visually it is very reminiscent of Leone's style, with gaunt images, bare dusty settings and cold-hearted violence.

An introduction to the films of Sergio Corbucci featuring the character of Django, and the westerns of Sergio Leone follows.

SERGIO CORBUCCI

b. 1927. d. 1990.

Corbucci made films in a wide variety of genres – many comedies, and also musicals, horrors and general adventure films. He made about 14 westerns but it is for two in particular, featuring the character of Django, that he has become internationally known. For the first he was the director. For the second, *Django 2*, or *Django Strikes Again* (*Django 2: il grande ritorno*), which Nello Rossati directed, he was one of the writers. The original film spawned many more 'Django' sequels, and in Germany any western featuring Franco Nero became known as a 'Django' film. Sergio's brother, Bruno Corbucci, was also a well-known director.

Django (1966)

Written by: Franco Rossetti, Jose G Maesso, Piero Vivarelli, Bruno Corbucci, Sergio Corbucci and Geoffrey Coppleston

Plot: While a battle is underway between Mexican and American soldiers in a small town on the border, a mysterious stranger called Django (Franco Nero) arrives in town. Everywhere the stranger goes he drags a coffin with him; nobody knows who or what is in it. A Major Jackson (Eduardo Fajardo) and his gang runs a protection racket to squeeze money out of the local people. His gang comes into confrontation with Django. A mercenary and old acquaintance of Django called Hugo Rodriguez (José Bodalò) arrives and they plan to rob a gold hoard from Jackson.

Comments: The film has an impressive and compelling opening sequence, with a man dragging a coffin through the desert and saving a woman from the attentions of some crooks. The film has become famous, indeed notorious, for its explicit violence.

SERGIO LEONE

b.1929. d. 1989.

Leone was surrounded by the world of Italian cinema from his birth. His father was one of the pioneers of Italian cinema, Roberto Roberti (also known as Vincenzo Leone), and his mother was actress Bice Waleram. Already as a teenager he was working as assistant director on films of Italian opera, such as *Rigoletto* (1946), *La Forza del Destino* and *Il Trovatore* (both in 1949), where doubtless he learned the fine art of presenting human figures in stylised groupings and in dramatic opposition to each other. He also had long experience working for American directors making Hollywood epics in Italy, such as *Quo Vadis* (1951), *Helen of Troy* (1956), *The Last Days of Pompeii* (1959) and *Ben Hur* (1959), which stood him in good stead when it came to creating his own cinematic mythology. Then from 1964 on he made the five westerns that created an entire sub-genre of the western with new perspectives on its conventions. They also made the name of Ennio Morricone, who composed the incidental music for all of them, internationally known. *Once Upon a Time in the West* (1968), generally considered to be his masterpiece, was not a success at the American box office. He turned down offers to direct *The Godfather* (1972) to work on the project that became *Once Upon a Time in America* (1984). When he died in 1989 he was preparing a co-production with Russia about the siege of Leningrad in World War Two.

A Fistful of Dollars (Per un pugno di dollari)(1964)

Written by: Sergio Leone, Victor Andréas Catena and Jaime Comas

Plot: A man with no name (Clint Eastwood) rides into a town which is torn apart by a feud between two families, the Baxters and the Rojos. He gets himself hired by both families and proceeds to set one family against the other. His sole motive in the whole enterprise is clearly money.

Comments: Essentially a remake of the Japanese director Akira Kurosawa's *Yojimbo* (1961), it came the year after the success of *The Magnificent Seven* (1960), a remake of Kurosawa's *Seven Samurai* (1954). The character of the man with no name is clearly conceived as a deliberate contrast to the traditional idealistic hero of the conventional western. Although he is ruthless and concerned only with monetary gain, we can admire him for his bravery and fighting skills. No one anticipated that the film would be popular in America at first, but its cynical amoral hero appealed to a new generation attuned to the brutalities of the world, through the country's involvement in the war in Vietnam. It also helped launch Clint Eastwood's career as a film actor, after his long-running appearances in the TV western series *Rawhide*.

For a Few Dollars More (Per qualche dollaro in più) (1965)

Written by: Luciano Vincenzoni

Plot: Two bounty hunters, one the 'Man with no Name' from *A Fistful of Dollars* (Clint Eastwood), the other Colonel Douglas Mortimer (Lee Van Cleef), are independently seeking the reward money for the killing of the bandit El Indio (Gian Maria Volonté). They then join forces in a rather untrusting alliance. The colonel also wants to kill El Indio out of personal revenge for his sister's death. When he succeeds in doing so, he allows the 'Man with no Name' to claim the reward.

Comments: Enormously popular at the box office, the plot of this sequel is more interesting and complex than its predecessor. It also features much bloody violence and has been criticised for its close-up studies of carnage.

The Good, the Bad and the Ugly (Il buono, il brutto, il cattivo) (1966)

Written by: Luciano Vincenzoni and Sergio Leone

Plot: During the Civil War a mysterious stranger known as Blondie (Clint Eastwood) saves the life of a Mexican bandit, Tuco (Eli Wallach), when he is captured by two bounty hunters. They form a partnership in which they agree to share the reward money for Tuco's capture, and the stranger rescues him from hanging. They're able to repeat this trick many times, with the reward money growing all the time. In a parallel story Sentenza (Lee Van Cleef) is trying to find some buried Confederate gold with the help of a gang of brutal thugs. Eventually, Tuco, the stranger and Sentenza join together in an uneasy alliance, which leads to betrayal and violence.

Comments: While Clint Eastwood reprises his performance from his two previous films for Leone, the strengths of the film lie in Lee Van Cleef's compelling performance and Eli Wallach's over-the-top charac-terisation of Tuco. The film is also memorable for its excessive violence, blood and gore. As with the others in the trilogy this film was more popular at the time with audiences than with critics, but has since come in for more favourable appraisal.

Once Upon a Time in the West (C'era una volta il West) (1968)

Written by: Sergio Donati, Bernardo Bertolucci, Dario Argento and Sergio Leone

Plot: A mysterious stranger with a harmonica (Charles Bronson) teams up with an outlaw called Cheyenne (Jason Robards) to protect a beautiful widow, Jill McBain (Claudia Cardinale), from a ruthless hired killer, Frank (Henry Fonda), who is working for a railroad boss.

Comments: The film quite deliberately introduces scenes of homage, parodying sequences from famous classic westerns, for example a stake-out like that in *High Noon* and action seen from the perspective of a young boy observing as in *Shane*. The whole culture of the West is in decay, with all the buildings, bars and people run-down and decrepit. Morricone's music was recorded before the film was shot, and specific themes identified with the main characters (on harmonica for the character played by Charles Bronson; on banjo for Cheyenne; and on strings for Jill McBain). The music was apparently played on the set so the actors could attune their performances to it.

A Fistful of Dynamite (Giù la testa) (1971)

Written by: Luciano Vincenzoni, Sergio Donati and Sergio Leone

Plot: A bandit, Juan Miranda (Rod Steiger), wants to rob a bank in a Mexican town but becomes involved in a revolution in which he has no interest. He meets up with John H Mallory (James Coburn) who is an IRA terrorist and an expert in explosives. At first Miranda hopes to enlist Mallory's help in robbing a bank in the Mesa Verde area, but Mallory attempts to do a deal with the revolutionaries and together they find themselves caught up in a peasant revolt.

Comments: Although the film contains some humorous moments, it is predominantly an action film. Of all Leone's 'spaghetti westerns', it provides the most rounded characters with complex motivation.

THE DEATH AND REBIRTH OF THE WESTERN

Film critics and theorists have attempted to pin labels on more recent developments in the genre of western films, particularly those made since the 1980s; and, on occasion, these labels have been applied retrospectively to films made prior to that decade which displayed some sense of 'self-reflexivity' or 'knowingness'. David Lusted (in his extensive and profound study 'The Western', 2003) has noted many such trends and categorised westerns accordingly. Thus he writes of 'elegiac westerns', 'revisionist westerns' (amongst which he includes a sub-category of 'revisionist epics' and the related 'environmentalist epics'), 'reflexive westerns', 'pro-Indian westerns', 'blaxploitation westerns', 'gangsta westerns', 'feminist westerns', 'modernist westerns', 'post-modernist westerns' and 'post-revisionist westerns'. Philip French, in his 'Westerns' (1977) made do with the all-encompassing term 'the post-western', and examined most of the same distinctions found by Lusted in his 'Westerns Revisited' (2004), in the chapters of the former work entitled 'Westward the Women', 'Legends Re-examined', 'The Modern West', and 'Transpositions and Displacements'. However, French managed on the whole without the jargon of cultural theory.

Whatever one's take on the westerns produced in the last 40 years or so, these films share something in common: they refuse to assume that any of the myths or literary and cinematic accounts of the settling of the West are unbiased. Conventions and presuppositions are questioned, and often reinterpreted, from perspectives commonly validated by present liberal and politically correct values. To some degree or other, all the concerns of the various schools of cultural theory, critical theory and literary theory are brought to bear, be it consciously or unconsciously, in both the creation of westerns and their evaluation. There is no such thing now, if indeed it ever existed, as a naïve western: all westerns are self-reflexive interpretations of their idiom.

With the film *Heaven's Gate* (1980) the western was presumed dead, quite simply because it was an epic western that failed at the box office. Yet it also marked the rebirth of the western in the sense that westerns now had to be successful as films irrespective of whether or not they were westerns. Producers could no longer assume that there was a 'westerns' audience out there, and so the self-reflexive western came of age. The films analysed in the following part of this chapter all exemplify these self-reflexive concerns, albeit in varying ways. It should be stressed that some of the films listed in chapter 5 on the 'Golden Age' can also be considered to be self-reflexive for reasons already discussed, but they have been included in that chapter because the bulk of the director's works sits more happily in that context. Some films considered in chapter 7, 'Other Gems', could also arguably be considered in the present chapter. The films listed below are in chronological order.

Little Big Man (1970)

Director: Arthur Penn
Written by: Calder Willingham

Plot: The film tells the life of a frontiersman, Jack Crabb (Dustin Hoffman), who is 121 years old. According to him he was brought up by Cheyenne Indians, survived the famous Custer's Last Stand, was familiar with Wild Bill Hickok, adopted as an Indian, and so on.

Comments: The storyteller is essentially recreating the myth of the Old West through his own life story, and often it is not at all clear where the borderlines are between the myths and factual history. In this respect the film reflects the nature of the American consciousness of its own past and the ambiguities inherent in the western genre. Thus, like the famous novel by Thomas Berger on which it is based, the film is an example of a revisionist treatment of the American West, but does not commit itself to a firm re-interpretation of that part of the country's history. There are, however, some clear revaluations. Wild Bill Hickok (Jeff Corey) appears as an amiable well-intentioned drinker, but General George Custer (Richard Mulligan) on the other hand is portrayed as an obsessive man, insensitive to the fate of his men. Although Dustin Hoffman won several awards for his performance (including the British BAFTA award for Best Actor), the most memorable performance in the film is Chief Dan George's as the Indian chief Old Lodge Skins.

McCabe and Mrs Miller (1971)

Director: Robert Altman
Written by: Robert Altman and Brian McKay

Plot: A gambler, John Q McCabe (Warren Beatty), opens a brothel in the town of Presbyterian Church on the Canadian border. An experienced madam of a brothel, Mrs Constance Miller (Julie Christie), offers to help him run the business. The business thrives but a large corporation tries to buy it out, and when McCabe refuses to let them they send gunmen to kill him.

Comments: The film displays the customary Altman characteristics: excessive visual detail, distracting cuts and zooms, and overlapping dialogue, which is at best incomprehensible and at worst inaudible. The film is certainly revisionist in its presentation of the life in a frontier town as generally unpleasant and undesirable. The characters are by and large unlikable, and hard to identify with sympathetically. The corporation is depicted as an evil force that dominates people's lives in Kafkaesque fashion. On the plus side its comedy is boisterous and its persistently experimental cinematography lends the film an interestingly surreal quality.

The Culpepper Cattle Company (1972)

Director: Dick Richards
Written by: Eric Bercovici and Gregory Prentiss

Plot: A teenage boy, Ben Mockridge (Gary Grimes), is hired by the hard, determined boss of the Culpepper Cattle Company, Frank Culpepper (Billy Green Bush). The boy joins him on a cattle drive to Colorado and learns how tough and violent such a drive can be.

Comments: The film is notable not only for a sensitive performance by the young Gary Grimes but also for attempting to depict the grim realities behind the romantic idealisations of cattle drives. It was the film debut of its director, Dick Richards, who had spent many years researching the history of the West prior to making the film.

The Life and Times of Judge Roy Bean (1972)

Director: John Huston
Written by: John Milius

Plot: The film relates the life of the infamous Judge Roy Bean (Paul Newman), focusing on important events. When Bean arrives in the town of Langtry in the Texas Badlands and finds himself on a wanted poster, he announces who he is in the local saloon, and is promptly beaten up. He is then tied to his horse and sent off into the prairie. He is saved by a Mexican girl (Victoria Principal), returns to the town and murders the townsfolk who drove him out. He sets up his own brand of law and order, dispensing justice with his guns.

Comments: The film is utterly disrespectful to the historical facts, making Bean a vengeful dispenser of dubious justice. Its saving grace is some good cameo performances by many of its all-star cast. Ava Gardner, for example, puts in a spirited performance as Lillie Langtry, the famed singer, to whom Bean acted as patron.

Revisionist it may be, but to what end?

Rooster Cogburn (1975)

Director: Stuart Millar
Written by: Martin Julien

Plot: The far from ideal dispenser of rough justice and heavy drinker Rooster Cogburn (John Wayne) has his marshal's badge removed by Judge Parker (John McIntire) for being too trigger-happy. But when a gang of outlaws attack a cavalry troop and steal their wagonload of arms, the judge offers to reinstate him if he can capture them. In the process Rooster meets up with the feisty Eula Goodnight (Katharine Hepburn) and her young Indian boy companion Wolf (Richard Romancito), and agrees to help her track down her father's killers.

Comments: John Wayne reprises his character from the Henry Hathaway film *True Grit* (1969). John Wayne's rough-hewn hero type is matched by an equally rough-hewn and determined female counterpart in the form of Eula Goodnight, played with rugged wilfulness by Katharine Hepburn, who rights the balance of traditionally male-dominated western narratives.

The Missouri Breaks (1976)

Director: Arthur Penn
Written by: Thomas McGuane

Plot: David Braxton (John McLiam) is a landowner who controls a large area where the rapids of the Missouri River break up the land (this being the origin of the title). Tom Logan (Jack Nicholson), leader of a gang of horse thieves, buys a ranch near Braxton's land. Logan pursues Braxton's daughter Jane (Kathleen Lloyd), who is disenchanted with her life. Braxton then employs a gunman, Robert E Lee Clayton (Marlon

Brando), to kill all members of Logan's gang.

Comments: The film is based on the historical Johnson County Wars in the 1890s when rich cattlemen hired gunmen to frighten away settlers. It culminates in scenes of disturbing violence with most of the principals being killed, apart from Logan and Jane. Marlon Brando made his character into a bizarre, camp and grotesque inversion of everything one associates with the western gunman: he disguises himself in women's clothes, is passionate about ornithology and complains about toothache, amongst other idiosyncrasies. Jack Nicholson's performance as Logan is also on the eccentric side: he seems to be as concerned about caring for his cabbages as he is about Braxton's daughter. The American Humane Association has included it on their list of 'unacceptable' films because many horses were severely injured in the making of the film, and one drowned.

The Shootist (1976)

Director: Don Siegel
Written by: Miles Hood Swarthout and Scott Hale

Plot: An aging gunfighter, John Bernard Books (John Wayne), known as 'The Shootist', visits a doctor (James Stewart) who confirms that he has cancer and will die in great pain. Books decides to end his days with dignity and in the spirit with which he has lived. He rents a room in the house of a widow, Bond Rogers (Lauren Bacall), and develops a warm relationship with her. Her son Gillom worships the old gunman and persuades him to give him a shooting lesson. Books works out a plan to stage a death for himself that will avoid the drawn out agony of a death from cancer. He sets up a confrontation with three men from his past who welcome the chance to outshoot a man they believe is too ill to beat them.

Comments: This is an elegy, if ever there was one, to the values of the Old West, in the figure of the sick, aging gunman. John Wayne plays the role with great dignity and sensitivity, providing a fitting and moving end to this his final film, and as memorable a swan song as any actor could wish.

Heaven's Gate (1980)

Director: Michael Cimino
Written by: Michael Cimino

Plot: During the Johnson County Wars in Wyoming in the 1890s a group of cattlemen, led by Frank Canton (Sam Waterston), draw up a list of 125 immigrant farmers from Eastern Europe who they consider to be responsible for cattle rustling. Sheriff James Averill (Kris Kristofferson) defends the interests of the farmers, but he clashes with a hired gunman, Nathan Champion (Christopher Walken).

Comments: When the film was first released, the critics in the popular press were almost unanimous in declaring it an unmitigated disaster, sounding the final death knell of the western genre. It undoubtedly does have many weaknesses, including a storyline that is often difficult to follow and a confusing mixture of historical facts and errors interwoven into a fictional plot. It was such a disaster at the box office that it led to the collapse of the studio that made it, United Artists, which was subsequently sold off to MGM. They had spent some $36 million on the film, a fortune in 1980. Much of the money spent can be considered unnecessary. An entire town was built in a remote area of Montana, and there was enormous expenditure on clothing for the extras to ensure historical accuracy. There are also many extensive set pieces in the film, such as the Harvard graduation near the beginning, which are self-indulgently long and add little real significance to the film. Even after 70 minutes were cut and it was re-released, the film fared no better. Its one achievement perhaps was to reverse the traditional view of the Johnson County wars, and in this sense it can be considered a revisionist western. In the novel 'The Virginian' of 1902, by Owen

Wister, of which several film versions and TV treatments were to be made, the wealthy cattlemen were considered right and the immigrant farmers unprincipled thieves. In *Heaven's Gate* the latter are portrayed as heroes for the cause of the poor, and as such the entire film becomes an account of class struggle in America.

The Long Riders (1980)

Director: Walter Hill
Written by: Bill Bryden, Steven Smith, James Keach and Stacy Keach

Plot: The film follows 15 years in the lives of the infamous James gang and their fellow outlaws. Their decision to turn to robbery is seen as motivated primarily by revenge. The raid on the Great Northfield Bank in Minnesota is depicted as a pivotal event in the lives of the robbers. When the gang's plans turn to chaos the James brothers decide to break up the gang.

Comments: The most remarkable aspect of this film is its use of four sets of related actors to play the four sets of brothers who made up the James gang. The actors in question are David, Keith and Robert Carradine; James and Stacy Keach; Dennis and Randy Quaid; and Christopher and Nicholas Guest. Knowing this somehow heightens the sense of realism in viewing the film. A thorough debunking of the romantic myth of the James brothers as Robin Hood figures, it depicts their lives as reckless and insecure, with Jesse's dream of domestic bliss cut brutally short. Most of the time the main characters look unkempt and travel-worn, hardly ever relinquishing the long coats, which earned them the name that provided the film with its title.

Silverado (1985)

Directed by: Lawrence Kasdan
Written by: Lawrence and Mark Kasdan

Plot: Paden (Kevin Kline) and Emmett (Scott Glenn) meet in the desert and decide to set out for the town of Silverado to confront the MacKendrick gang. On the way they help Emmett's brother Jake (Kevin Costner) to escape from gaol by tricking the sheriff, John T Langston (John Cleese). They are then joined by a black man, Malachi Johnson (Danny Glover), who is trying to find his family. On arrival at Silverado they have to deal with the corrupt sheriff, Cobb (Brian Dennehy), who is in the pay of the true villain of the piece, MacKendrick.

Comments: A disparate group of actors play an odd assortment of travelling partners. It comes as a special surprise to find British comedy star John Cleese playing a sheriff in a western. The director has also made the film very much a family affair. Production, direction and script bear the Kasdan name, but also several bit parts: check the cast list and you will find a Jon Kasdan playing a boy at an outpost, a Meg Kasdan as a barmaid in a saloon, and a Jake Kasdan as a stable boy. The film incorporates many of the traditional themes and character types of the genre, but presents them with consistent irony. Director and actors have conspired to invite the audience to knowingly observe how they are playing with conventions. In this it provides a postmodern perspective. (See also Chapter 11)

Pale Rider (1985)

Note: For plot and comments, see under Clint Eastwood in Chapter 5.

Dances with Wolves (1990)

Director: Kevin Costner
Written by: Michael Blake

Plot: Lieutenant John Dunbar (Kevin Costner) is an officer in the Union army during the Civil War in the 1860s. When given a frontier post he befriends a wolf and becomes involved in the lives of the Sioux Indians. He is so attracted by their life and attitudes to Nature and the spirit world that he stays with them and adopts a Sioux name, which translates as 'Dances with Wolves'.

Comments: This was Kevin Costner's first film as director, and it boasts some beautiful cinematography and a memorable musical score by John Barry. It is at fault though for historical inaccuracy and an over-righteous political correctness. Virtually all the white men in the film, apart from Dunbar, are cruel, stupid and possibly mad, while the Sioux Indians appear as the only ones in touch with their true selves. The Pawnee Indians are shown to be hell-bent on exterminating the Sioux, while historically the opposite was true. The film was very popular and won six Academy Awards.

Unforgiven (1992)

Note: for plot and comments see under Clint Eastwood in chapter 5 and chapter 11 for an extensive analysis.

The Last of the Mohicans (1992)

Director: Michael Mann
Written by: Michael Mann and Christopher Crowe

Plot: Set in colonial times, with the French and British at war, Hawkeye (Daniel Day-Lewis), together with a couple of Mohican Indians, escorts two sisters, Alice and Cora Monroe, through wild territory to join their father, the British commander of soldiers who are being besieged by the French.

Comments: This is the seventh known film version of James Fenimore Cooper's famous novel. In 1909 DW Griffith adapted it loosely as *Leatherstocking*. Then there were two one-reeler versions within the same year, 1911, and in 1920 there was a six-reel version directed by Maurice Tourneur and Clarence Brown, starring Wallace Beery as the Huron warrior Magua, with Hawkeye as a secondary figure. The first sound version in 1932 was made as a serial and starred Harry Carey. The version by George Seitz in 1936 starred Randolph Scott as Hawkeye. Michael Mann's version romanticises the figure of Hawkeye considerably and provides impressive and bloody battle scenes in accordance with the prevailing taste at the time for convincing violence.

Geronimo: An American Legend (1993)

Director: Walter Hill
Written by: John Milius and Larry Gross

Plot: The film charts the attempts made by the US army from 1885 to 1886 to put a final stop to the Indian uprisings, focusing in on the confrontations with the Indian chief Geronimo. The Apaches have agreed reluctantly to settle on the reservation imposed on them by the US government, but many cannot adapt to the changes in lifestyle this entails. Geronimo constantly manages to evade capture.

Comments: The film presents an honest and frank view of the treatment of the Apaches without polarising the issues in terms of 'goodies' and 'baddies', though there is clear sympathy for the plight of Geronimo. There are strong, convincing performances in all the major roles (Gene Hackman, Robert Duvall and Matt Damon) with a particularly powerful performance by Wes Studi as Geronimo.

Posse (1993)

Director: Mario van Peebles
Written by: Sy Richardson and Dario Scardapane

Plot: A black infantryman (Mario van Peebles) leads fellow soldiers in revolt against a group, led by his former commanding officer, who believe in the supremacy of whites.
　　Comments: The film grafts the issue of race relations onto a conventional revenge plot.

Tombstone (1993)

Director: George Cosmatos
Written by: Kevin Jarre and John Fasano

Plot: The famous marshal of Dodge City Wyatt Earp (Kurt Russell) has retired and hopes for a more peaceful life in Tombstone. He meets up with his brothers Morgan (Bill Paxton) and Virgil (Sam Elliott), as well as the consumptive Doc Holliday (Val Kilmer). The film follows the sequence of events that lead up to the famous gunfight at the OK Corral, with the Clanton gang.
　　Comments: The director has aimed for some historical accuracy, making, for example, Virgil the leader of the Earp family. The film is perhaps most memorable for an over-the-top performance as Doc Holliday by Val Kilmer.

The Ballad of Little Jo (1993)

Director: Maggie Greenwald
Written by: Maggie Greenwald

Plot: Josephine Monaghan (Suzy Amis) gives birth to an illegitimate child and flees from New England with its conservative values to the West. She discovers, however, that the only work she can find there as a single mother is as a prostitute, so she decides to pass herself off as a man.

Comments: The film is based on a true story set during the Gold Rush of 1366. It reinterprets the conventions of the genre from a feminist standpoint. The result is a serious, thought-provoking film.

Wyatt Earp (1994)

Director: Lawrence Kasdan
Written by: Dan Gordon and Lawrence Kasdan

Plot: The film tells the life of Wyatt Earp (Kevin Costner) from his birth, through his childhood in Iowa, joining his father's law practice, working for Wells Fargo and becoming a US marshal.

Comments: Despite an excellent cast the film never really comes dramatically alive and suffers from its slow, tedious pace. In its attempt to be thoroughly and historically accurate it has simply included too much detail. There are several examples of bad language and some crude sexual innuendoes, which, while they may contribute to the sense of realism, do nothing to heighten the drama. Dennis Quaid, who lost weight and grew a moustache for the part, is almost unrecognisable as Doc Holliday.

Legends of the Fall (1994)

Director: Edward Zwick
Written by: Susan Shilliday and Bill Wittliff

Plot: The story is set in Montana, in the remote Rocky Mountains, during the early twentieth century, and concerns the lives of three sons of a retired cavalry officer, Colonel Ludlow (Anthony Hopkins). He deliberately brings them up far away from the life and society he has come to despise. The relationship between the three brothers is very close until Samuel (Henry Thomas), the youngest, returns from college with his beautiful fiancée, Susannah (Julia Ormond). The eldest son, Alfred (Aidan Quinn), begins to fall in love with her, and to add to the complications a passionate relationship develops between Susannah and the third brother, Tristan (Brad Pitt). As they become involved in fighting in World War One, the relationships between the three brothers are torn apart.

Comments: What promises to be a saga develops into melodrama, but the film is maintained by strong performances from all the principals and gorgeous scenery. It contains a basically pessimistic vision: that any attempt to recreate artificially an idyllic state of innocence is doomed to failure, for desire and worldly conflicts will inevitably intrude. In this sense the film echoes the bitter experiences of the original pioneers and settlers of the West, but in a setting that is not so remote from the present.

Bad Girls (1994)

Director: Jonathan Kaplan
Written by: Yolande Finch and Ken Friedman

Plot: Four prostitutes leave Colorado in search of a better life after a shooting in a brothel. Cody Zamora (Madeleine Stowe) kills a client of a fellow prostitute, Anita (Mary Stuart Masterson), when he abuses her. Together with Eileen (Andie MacDowell) and Lilly (Drew Barrymore) they escape to Texas pursued by two detectives, Graves (Jim Beaver) and O'Brady (Nick Chinlund), from the Pinkerton agency. The women imitate the tough ways of men, toting guns, and find themselves challenged to prove their mettle when Cody has her money stolen by her former lover Kid Jarrett.

Comments: Originally Tamra Davis was slated to direct the film but the production company weren't keen on how she was developing it so replaced her with Jonathan Kaplan. Whatever the original aims of director and writer, the result is a film that tries to make a feminist statement about the West but ends up confirming all its stereotypes; a time when all males were macho and all independent women prostitutes.

Pocahontas (1995)

Directors: Mike Gabriel and Eric Goldberg
Written by: Carl Binder, Chris Buck and others
Voice actors: Irene Bedard, Mel Gibson, David Ogden Stiers, John Kassir, etc.

Plot: Pocahontas, the daughter of Chief Powhatan, is pledged to marry her tribe's greatest warrior, but, after seeing a vision of a spinning arrow, she believes that her life will be greatly changed. One day an English ship arrives carrying Governor Ratcliffe who is bent on plundering the New World with the aid of a band of soldiers and sailors under the leadership of John Smith. Smith and Pocahontas have to join forces to try and prevent conflict between the unprincipled Ratcliffe and the rightfully suspicious Powhatan.

Comments: The Disney company had hoped that this animated version of the legend would equal the success of *The Lion King* (1994), but its serious adult themes seem not to have attracted young audiences. All the delights of expert animation are there together with romantic visionary songs, and music by Alan Menken, which create an idealisation of both legend and history. The focus on the role of a Native American woman in her attempts to bring peace to her known world was timely in the mid-1990s. The film is not strictly a western, but explores shared cultural roots.

Wild Bill (1995)

Director: Walter Hill
Written by: Walter Hill

Plot: The life of 'Wild Bill' Hickok (Jeff Bridges), the famous gunman and lawman, is told in flashbacks as he awaits, in Deadwood, South Dakota, the arrival of a mysterious stranger, Jack McCall (David Arquette), who has announced that he will not leave until Hickok is dead.

Comments: Basing the screenplay partly on the novel 'Deadwood' by Pete Dexter and the play 'Fathers and Son' by Thomas Babe, the director, who also wrote the screenplay, has added his own romantic twists to the story. He has Hickok carry on an affair with Calamity Jane (Ellen Barkin) and includes a lost love, Susannah (Diane Lane), the mother of the man stalking him, who himself may be Hickok's own son. He also manages to weave Buffalo Bill Cody (Keith Carradine) into the plot. The film provides the most thorough debunking of the legend that one could imagine, stressing Hickok's addiction to alcohol, his near blindness and syphilis. The audience is distanced from events by the narration of an Englishman called Charley (John Hurt), and over-exposure and manipulation of visual images creates a deliberate dream-like quality in some of the scenes.

Dead Man (1995)

B&W.
Director: Jim Jarmusch
Written by: Jim Jarmusch

Plot: A quiet accountant from Ohio, Bill Blake (Johnny Depp), leaves his job in Cleveland to work in the West and is gradually transformed into a notorious gunman.

Comments: A richly complex western with allusions galore to other westerns, conventions of the genre, and historical realities. Constantly questions, by way of postmodernism, the whole notion of fixed meaning.

Lone Star (1996)

Director: John Sayles
Written by: John Sayles

Plot: Sam Deeds (Chris Cooper) is a sheriff in Rio County, Texas, who investigates a 40-year-old skeleton found in the desert. While trying to solve this old murder he discovers more about his own father, who used to be sheriff too, and reawakens his interest in an old flame from his school days.

Comments: A fascinating and complex murder mystery that just happens to be a good western too. Acting is sensitive throughout and the film remains compelling to the last. Its revisionist element is in its treatment of the theme of law and order.

The Hi-Lo Country (1998)

Director: Stephen Frears
Written by: Walon Green

Plot: The film focuses on the strong bond of friendship between two men, the introspective Pete (Billy Crudup) and the boisterous Big Boy (Woody Harrelson), in what remains of the Old West after the Second World War. A well-to-do landowner called Jim Ed Love (Sam Elliot) wants to buy their land, but they refuse. They join forces with another rancher (James Gammon), so that they can drive cattle to the railheads in the traditional way. The men live and work on the prairie, where they feel truly at home, but they are not so at ease in dealing with affairs of the heart.

Comments: It is difficult to justify calling this film a western because of the period in which it is set, but the main elements of the plot set it firmly in the genre. It also brings out both the attractions of the cowboy lifestyle and its rather limited social aspects.

Ride with the Devil (1999)

Director: Ang Lee
Written by: James Schamus

Plot: The film focuses on the lives of Jake Roedel (Tobey Maguire) and Jack Bull Chiles (Skeet Ulrich) at the outbreak of the Civil War. When Jack's father is killed by Union soldiers, the young men join a group of irregular fighters supporting the cause of the South. Hiding after a fight, the two friends are brought food by a young widow, and she and Jack become lovers, but he is seriously wounded and Jake helps her get away to a safe farm. As more of his friends die Jake becomes disenchanted with the war.

    Comments: A film about war that refuses to take obvious sides, with human motivation that is often ambiguous. Rather than fighting to preserve or abolish slavery it appears that most people are involved in the war to gain their own personal freedom.

Wild Wild West (1999)

Director: Barry Sonnenfeld
Written by: SS Wilson, Brent Maddock and others

Plot: Set during the Civil War, President Ulysses Grant (Kevin Kline) employs a former war hero Jim West (Will Smith) and a US marshal, Artemus Gordon (Kevin Kline again), a master of disguises, to capture a dangerous and mad Confederate, Arliss Loveless (Kenneth Branagh), who is planning to assassinate the president. The central part of the film is set on a train journey from Washington to Utah, where West and Gordon do battle with the mad Loveless.

Comments: Despite employing a large number of scriptwriters, most of the gags in this would-be comedy misfire. The western setting and the context of the Civil War are gratuitous, and little is gained in this instance by imposing a very modern sense of the zany onto a fantasy Wild West.

All the Pretty Horses (2000)

Director: Billy Bob Thornton
Written by: Ted Tally

Plot: Two young Texan cowboys ride into Mexico in search of new experiences. While they find the country beautiful, they also discover that it is mysterious and threatening.

Comments: Thornton is a devotee of measured pacing, and this one drags a little too slowly for the patience of the average audience. Nevertheless it repays careful study: there are subtle performances creating complex psychological webs (by Matt Damon, Henry Thomas and Penélope Cruz in the leads).

The Missing (2003)

Director: Ron Howard
Written by: Ken Kaufman

Plot: Set in New Mexico in 1885. Samuel Jones (Tommy Lee Jones) returns home, hoping to reestablish a good relationship with his estranged adult daughter Maggie (Cate Blanchett). When Maggie's own daughter is kidnapped by an Apache, father and daughter have to work together to get her back.

Comments: A thriller first and a western second. A strength of the film is the mesmerising performance by Eric Schweig as an Apache witch doctor.

Open Range (2003)

Director: Kevin Costner
Written by: Craig Storper

Plot: Grazing their cattle on the prairies, four men, Boss Spearman (Robert Duvall), Charley Waite (Kevin Costner), Mose Harrison (Abraham Benrubi) and Button (Diego Luna), a 16-year-old Spanish boy, share friendship and common values. When they are near the small town of Harmonville, they meet up with a corrupt sheriff (James Russo) and a ranch owner (Michael Gambon) who controls the district through installing fear in those who live there. Boss and Charley are drawn into defending themselves and their way of life against the ranch owner.

Comments: The film utilises a well-worn situation of the genre: outsiders solving the problems of a community dominated by cruel landowners. What raises it above the conventional is the opposition between the notion of land control and containment on the one hand and that of a life of free-roaming individualism on the other. The personalities of the four main characters are also explored in much greater depth than in many a western, but not through explicit discussion so much as implication in finely written elliptical dialogue.

Cold Mountain (2003)

Director: Anthony Minghella
Written by: Anthony Minghella

Plot: The film tells of a wounded Confederate soldier called Inman (Jude Law) in the final days of the Civil War, who sets out on a perilous journey to find his way home to Cold Mountain, North Carolina, and rejoin the woman he loves, Ada (Nicole Kidman). On the way he meets a range of odd and interesting people, while back home Ada is learning how to look after the farm now that her father is dead, with the aid of an unusual but practical woman called Ruby (Renée Zellweger).

Comments: The parallels with Homer's Odyssey are clear, though Inman is in the non-heroic mould, and in fact a deserter. The landscapes are hauntingly beautiful, and stay in the memory long after details of the plot. The film achieves a remarkable feat by having the Civil War as central to its meaning but keeping the action of it mostly at a distance.

The Last Samurai (2003)

Director: Edward Zwick
Written by: John Logan, Edward Zwick and Marshall Herskovitz

Plot: A veteran of the Civil War, Captain Nathan Algren (Tom Cruise) is hired by some American businessmen who are trying to obtain lucrative contracts from the Japanese Emperor. His mission is to train Japanese peasants in the use of guns for the imperial army because the Japanese government wish to suppress a rebellion of Samurai warriors who are rejecting new attempts at westernisation. Algren, who is badly wounded in fighting, has his life spared by the Samurai leader Katsumoto (Ken Watanabe), and he gradually learns to respect the Samurai traditions. He is then faced with loyalty dilemma when he has to return to the battle-field.

Comments: At the centre of this eastern western is a man who finds himself neither here nor there. He is torn between tradition and modernity, between eastern culture and the western (in both the narrower and broader meaning) values he was brought up to respect. The film presents an odd juxtaposition of different myths, that of the American West with that of the Samurai warriors of Japan. The audience is clearly being invited to compare and contrast. In one sense the American Civil War was fought against feudalist notions of one part of humanity being in slavery to the other, while in Japan feudalism was struggling to coexist with the new.

The Alamo (2004)

Director: John Lee Hancock
Written by: Leslie Bohem, Stephen Gaghan and John Lee Hancock

Plot: The film focuses on the famous siege of the Alamo, an abandoned mission house, in 1836, where 183 Texans and Mexican-born Texans are under the command of Colonel Travis (Patrick Wilson). Among those besieged there by the army of the Mexican General Santa Anna (Emilio Echevarría) are Davy Crockett (Billy Bob Thornton) and Jim Bowie (Jason Patric). The film also includes the conflict between the small army of Texans, led by General Sam Houston (Dennis Quaid), and that of Santa Anna at the subsequent battle of San Jacinto, which Houston's army won, leading to the independence of Texas.

Comments: The director took great pains to ensure historical accuracy, and this is the film's main virtue. Little can be faulted concerning costume, guns, the unfolding of events, end even meteorological conditions. There are strong performances from the leading actors, but little attempt to interpret events in any serious way.

Hidalgo (2004)

Director: Joe Johnston
Written by: John Fusco

Plot: In 1890 a wealthy Arabian sheik invites the American Frank T Hopkins (played in the film by Viggo Mortensen) to enter his horse, a mustang named Hidalgo, for the famous 'Ocean of Fire' race over 3,000 miles of the Arabian Desert. The race has been held yearly for centuries and restricted only to thoroughbred horses owned by Arab royal families. Hopkins is regarded by many as the greatest rider in the West. He has been both cowboy and dispatch rider to the US Cavalry. Some Arabs are determined to prevent him winning, and for Hopkins it becomes a matter of national and personal pride.

Comments: The link between the main story about the Arabian horse race and the American West is tenuous, but it is there. At the beginning of the film there is a sequence showing the famous massacre of Indians at Wounded Knee, with Chief Big Foot lying dead. It is revealed in the film that Hopkins, who witnesses the massacre, is half Indian. For a while he performs with his horse in Buffalo Bill's Wild West Show, but tires of humiliating himself in this fashion. The invitation to race in Arabia is thus seen as a chance of fulfilment that he could never achieve in his native land.

Brokeback Mountain (2005)

Director: Ang Lee
Written by: Larry McMurtry and Diana Ossana

Plot: Two young men, a ranch hand, Ennis Del Mar (Heath Ledger), and a rodeo cowboy, Jack Twist (Jake Gyllenhaal), meet in the summer of 1963 to work together herding sheep or the high mountain pastures of Wyoming. The taciturn Ennis learns to come out of himself and Jack initiates a relationship between them which becomes a deep and passionate affair. They only consummate their love every time they go on fishing trips together away from their wives and families. Social pressures against homosexual relationships in general and family obligations in the case of Ennis make it difficult to maintain the affair, which ends tragically, but with confirmation of the power of love.

Comments: Is it a western? It has been talked of as the first 'gay western', but it has few of the trappings of the genre. It is set in the West certainly, but in the 1960s. The two central characters are not truly cowboys, but shepherds. There is some precedent for this aspect, however, in the film *The Sheepman* (1958) with Glenn Ford. The two main characters certainly look like cowboys, complete with stetsons, jeans and horses. The film bears only a superficial likeness to any traditional westerns yet depends for its full effect on familiarity with the values and prejudices of the traditional West. Joe Aguirre (Randy Quaid), the two men's boss while they are on the mountain pasture, makes quite clear when Jack returns the following summer that there are no jobs available for gay men, and Jack eventually dies as a result of homophobic hatred, in a manner similar to that which Ennis witnessed as a child. In the West, it seems, a man still has to be a man, or perish. Jack's own father is clearly disgusted and ashamed at what he knows his son to be. Only his mother perceives the genuine love that is manifest in Ennis for her son. The film was based on a short story by Annie Proulx.

SOME MODERN CLASSICS

This chapter comprises analyses of three recent westerns that have acquired the status of modern classics. In each case only the title, date and director's name is given. Plot summaries and other comments can be found under the title of the film in Chapters 5 and 10.

The Wild Bunch (1969)

Director: Sam Peckinpah

Not so much wild as feral. At some stage of their existence, a group of men have led a semblance of a normal life, and been involved in relationships that subsequently failed. For years they have been bound together by the desire to reap sufficient riches from armed robbery to enable them to give it all up and retire. Now it really is getting rather late in the day, especially for Pike Bishop (William Holden) and Dutch Engstrom (Ernest Borgnine). It is easy to warm to their vulnerable humanity, and yet they are merciless killers, who massacre on a large scale, without any qualms. Therein lies the challenging paradox of Sam Peckinpah's film, praiseworthy for its psychological finesse and condemned for excessive and gratuitous violence.

This divide between consciousness of humanity and the rationalised unfeeling ability to slaughter is one of the central themes of the film. From the behaviour of the main characters one could draw the conclusion that psychosis is the normal condition of mankind. Human beings compartmentalise their experiences, feelings and wishes, allowing incompatible thoughts to co-exist. The opening sequence of the film makes this abundantly clear. A group of men in brown uniforms (later identifiable as army uniforms) ride at a steady pace into a town. On their way they pass a group of children amusing themselves by putting two scorpions amidst a mass of ants. Violence is portrayed as an essential part of the natural process. The ants attack the defenceless scorpions mercilessly. The further perspective on this is that the children watch it all with obvious glee. It seems natural that they enjoy the spectacle of violence until they learn to temper that enjoyment with conscious and moral categorisation.

Soon after this one of the men in uniform (whom we can later identify as Pike) collides with an old lady carrying parcels. He apologises and helps her, establishing the human side of Pike's character. Then it becomes obvious that the gang's purpose is to rob the bank, and they hold up all the staff at gunpoint. Pike says unequivocally, coldly, 'If they move, kill 'em' – kindness and merciless violence co-existing. The gang wait for the right moment, so that they can escape under cover of a march by a local Temperance Society. Meanwhile a posse, of sorts, is stalking them. The railroad boss, whose company the gang have previously robbed, has employed Deke Thornton (Robert Ryan), together with a gang of rather incompetent helpers, to catch Pike and his gang, dead or alive. It comes to a shoot-out, with many of Deke's men on the rooftops and Pike's men still inside the bank. Neither group care very much about the fate of the Temperance Society marching between them, and slaughter occurs. Three incidents confirm Pike's ability to dissociate from the personal in order to survive. In order to escape from the bank, he pushes the clerk forward and orders his men, 'When I kick him out, blast him. We'll make a run for it'. He leaves a young man behind to keep the employees at gunpoint, and make Deke think that they are still in the bank. The young man is naïve enough to do this without question. Eventually he loses his cool and shoots them as they try to escape, thus alerting Deke's men. Later we discover that he was the grandson of Freddie Sykes (Edmond O'Brien), the old man who was left in charge of the horses. Pike keeps quiet about his fate. Then, just after leaving town, one of the gang is too badly wounded in the head to continue. He begs Pike to 'finish it'. Pike does not even hesitate, but shoots him at once, as if he were a wounded animal. As the gang leave the town, there is a shot of the children again, playing with the scorpions and the ants. This time the children put straw on the creatures and set fire to it.

Violence seen from the child's perspective occurs at various other stages in the film. After the massacre they run around shouting 'Bang!' replaying the event as a game. And in the final shoot-out at Ague Verde, groups of children look on. It is difficult to interpret the gaze: is it horror or fascination, or both? In fact the only part of the film in which children look innocently happy is in the idyllic interlude in the home village of the young Mexican gang member, Angel (Jaime Sanchez). Deke's men also behave very much like children: after the first massacre and the final debacle, they run around shouting to each other in glee at the number of bodies, robbing them of what is valuable. Pike's men too, in moments of relief, after an escape or after a crisis, frequently indulge themselves in childish laughter at some silly joke or other. It becomes almost predictable. Even Deke, at the end, when old Freddie invites him to join him, laughs at the absurdity of it all. The importance of the child's perspective is expressed most explicitly in the words of the old man in Angel's village: 'We all dream of being a child again, even the worst of us, perhaps the worst most of all'.

There are several sequences in the film when the main characters reflect about their lives and hopes for the future, marking the differences between the attitudes of Pike and Dutch. They agree on aspects of their approaching old age; in Pike's words, 'These days are closing fast'. Whereas Pike envisages a peaceful old age, however ('I'd like to make a good score and then back off'), Dutch replies, 'Back off to what?' Dutch is in this respect more of a realist. They also differ on the matter of trust. Pike is willing to trust a man's word, but Dutch almost loses his temper when Pike mentions this. For him it is not the fact that you give your trust that is important, 'It's who you give it to!' They both agree, however, that one should have no regrets. Wrapped in their blankets at night, Pike adds: 'I wouldn't have it any other way'. And before turning over to sleep, Dutch says, 'Pike... I wouldn't have it any other way either'. This scene reveals the companionship that is important to both of them, on a personal level and as a prerequisite of their own safety. Pike is adamant about it: 'We've got to stick by each other'. Later in the film he comments, 'We started together. We end together'. Without any explicit hint of homoeroticism, there is a clear indication that for Dutch the relationship with Pike is the most important in his life. When the other men indulge themselves in whoring in Ague Verde, he stays outside. When he sees that Pike has been mortally wounded at the end he cries, 'Pike, no!' and his dying utterance is 'Pike...'

Deke's relationship to the gang is an intriguing one. He does miss such companionship, which the incompetent band under his command cannot provide. Several times he expresses the wish that he were with Pike and his men, instead of pursuing them ('I wish to God I were with them', for example). This is certainly one of the reasons he agrees to go with old Freddie at the end, when all the others are dead. Freddie's promise is the best offer he is likely to get: 'It can't be like it used to be, but it'll do'.

There are several aspects of the film, which put the events into historical perspective. When the gang meets the self-styled General Mapache (Emilio Fernández) in Agua Verde, he is accompanied by an officer of the German Imperial Army, Commander Frederick Mohr (Fernando Wagner), who shows interest in this group of Americans who seem to oppose the policies of their own government. When Mapache arrives in a bright red automobile, it is clear that most of the gang have never seen such a contraption before. Pike confirms, however, that he has heard that they started to make them with wings: 'The government will use them in the war, they say'. Such details serve to emphasise that

Pike and his like are fast becoming historical relics.

A high point in the film when it comes to action is the raid on the arms train, ingeniously planned by Pike, with his men concealed cleverly in unlikely places: under the rails in a culvert, inside the pipe of a water storage tank, and so on. There's comedy here also at the expense of the raw young soldiers accompanying the arms shipment, who are so confused that they cannot get their horses off the train properly.

In the bloodbath, in which almost everyone gets killed apart from Deke, his men and old Freddie, it is as if Pike and his gang know this is the final showdown (what can they 'back off' to?). They march in a line into the town square and demand that Angel be returned to them. It is true that the shooting spree is provoked by the General, who at first offers Angel but then cuts his throat, but it seems like a pretext. There is one drawn-out hiatus, when it seems that there is a last chance to prevent general bloodshed, but Pike spots an officer (it looks like the German in dress uniform) and shoots him. From then on all hell breaks loose.

If there is any sense of justice being meted out at the end of the film, then it is predominantly poetic justice. They all die as they have lived ('I wouldn't have it any other way').

Silverado (1985)

Director: Lawrence Kasdan

Silverado is a well-rounded film, the loose ends of which are neatly tied up by the end, and brought to bear on its central themes. All the couples and a family are reunited happily, as usually occurs before the curtain falls in a Shakespearean comedy. Indeed, comparisons can be made to Shakespeare's darker comedies.

The threat of death and the notion of comedy are near allied in the compelling opening sequence of the film. From a pan across a quiet, dark and dusty room, with a stove, a pile of wood, a saddle, and a man sleeping, we, as is he, are shocked into consciousness that someone is violently attacking this fragile structure from outside. Wood splinters, holes appear, bullets fly. The man shoots desperately through the flimsy walls, till there is silence outside. One man is dead but others have fled. A piebald horse remains with a double-diamond brand on its flank, one of the details that we quickly forget about until later in the film. He sets off on one horse, trailing the others, and finds another man, lying neatly in the desert, in nothing but bright pink long underwear. He gives the man some water. It is the start of a long friendship. Here already an element of the absurd is beginning to enter into the plot (a man in pink underwear in the middle of the desert?). The first man is later identified as Emmett (Scott Glenn) and the second as Paden (Kevin Kline). Emmett has the first (of many) good one-liners in the film. On being asked by Paden, 'They just jumped you out of the blue?' he replies, 'I had to get up anyway'. It turns out that Paden has been jumped too, and he is more concerned about the loss of his stylish hat than anything else.

In a cavalry fort they meet up with two of Paden's old riding buddies, Cobb (Brian Dennehy) and Tyree (Jeff Fahey), both of whom ask Paden, 'Where's the dog?' This is the second detail of which the significance becomes clear only later in the film. They travel to the township of Turley to meet up with Emmett's brother Jake (Kevin Costner), and go on to the larger town of Silverado to see their sister Kate and her family, with the ultimate intention of going on to California. Paden tries to remain aloof but finds himself increasingly drawn into helping them and their family.

At Turley, the film continues to tread the fine line between farce and tragedy. Jake is in jail for 'kissing a girl' (and shooting someone as a result). Paden ends up being thrown in jail with Jake for shooting the man who stole his hat. Saloons, Paden admits several times, are his element: 'A good smelly saloon is my favourite place in the world'. It is in the saloon in Turley that an incident occurs which starts the subplot in the film. A black man, Mal (Danny Glover), arrives and orders a drink. He is told in no uncertain terms that his kind are not welcome. Enter John Cleese in a beard. More like a nineteenth-century London peeler than a western sheriff he asks, 'What's all this then?' After ineffective protests, Mal is promptly ordered out of the town. Another plotline has been set up as Emmett and Paden first arrive in the town, when they are confused with two men called Baxter and Hawley by the leader of a wagon train to Silverado, who rather unwisely displays the large amount of money he is carrying in a chest.

Their departure from Turley is more hurried than their arrival. Emmett has arranged to free his brother and Paden from jail, to avoid a hanging. He sets the gallows on fire to distract the townsfolk and the sheriff, while Jake and Paden employ a hilarious ruse to fool the deputy on guard and relieve him of his keys. Once they're safely away the three meet up with Mal and the four ride together (accompanied by suitably heroic music). They eventually catch up with the wagon train, where everyone is depressed, as Baxter and Hawley have made off with the chest of money, which they need to set up their homesteads near Silverado. The 'magnificent four' (or perhaps, more appropriately, the 'four amigos') save the day, track down the thieves and return the money to the wagon train. Paden has become fond of a woman whose husband has just been killed. While Mal goes off for a while to seek his family (later to rejoin the main plot), Paden becomes rather disenchanted with the widow and her intense pioneering spirit. She is beautiful, but life with her seems like hard work. She proclaims to him: 'I want to build something, make things grow. That takes a lifetime'.

The scene that gets to the heart of the film's serious message takes place between Mal and his old father, forced to live on a hillside after his house has been razed to the ground by the henchmen of the local cattle owner MacKendrick. 'What about the law?' asks Mal. 'What law? The law runs a man down', replies his father. 'That ain't right. I had enough of what ain't right', concludes Mal. Mal also learns that his sister Rae has become a loose woman in the town, and shortly after Mal finds his father killed and is later able to identify his father's rifle in the hands of one of MacKendrick's men.

The issue that affects Mal's father also affects the would-be settlers on the wagon train. They have bought land legally to set up farms, but MacKendrick and his like insist that all the land is free for the grazing of cattle (a frequent occasion for conflict in westerns).

The law in Silverado is basically the will of one person: Sheriff Cobb. Later it is revealed, in a telling scene in the sheriff's office, that he is subservient to MacKendrick. When Cobb encounters Paden again in the saloon he says, 'Welcome to Heaven'. It is for him. He runs the town by exploiting people's weaknesses and through instigating fear.

It is at this stage that the various elements of the plot begin to coalesce. The significance of the double-diamond brand and the reference to Paden's dog become clear. Emmett had killed the father of MacKendrick for which he had served a prison sentence. On taking over his father's cattle empire the younger MacKendrick had changed the family brand to… a double-diamond. It is thus clear that the men who attacked Emmett in the opening scene of the film were MacKendrick's men seeking revenge.

The allusion to a dog refers to an occasion when Paden was more concerned about an injured dog than his own escape and got himself arrested. This is a weakness that Cobb now utilises. Paden has become fond of the most original character in the film, Stella, the manageress of 'The Midnight Star' saloon. It's an unusual role beautifully played by Linda Hunt. At around four foot tall, she has invented an ingenious slope and platform behind the bar which enables her to serve at the bar at normal height. Cobb is able to force Paden to stay out of the conflict with Jake and Emmett because of his sympathy for her. Paden can no longer stay aloof, however, when Cobb allows MacKendrick's men to shoot Emmet's and Jake's brother-in-law and kidnap their nephew, burning the house in the process. After several more twists and turns in the plot, MacKendrick and his men get their comeuppance and the stage is set for a classic confrontation between Paden and Cobb on the main street.

Treading a fine line between farce and tragedy, the film is tongue in cheek one moment, only to have you tense with suspense the next. In a sense it's postmodern, and everyone involved in the production seems to think it's impossible to work within the conventions of the western genre without displaying a critical awareness of those conventions. Yet the film isn't a parody; it doesn't mock. It is an affectionate look back at a genre, with music that's very much in the vein of the great western film scores of the past: great striding brass, evoking wide landscapes and myth. It has a fairytale ending, with optimistic prospects promised for all the main characters. Unusually, there's not a Native American in sight.

Unforgiven (1992)

Director: Clint Eastwood

Who then are the unforgiven in this film? Certainly the two cowboys, one of whom mutilated a prostitute and the other who tried to help him escape. Also Sheriff Little Bill (Gene Hackman), who tortured the negro Ned (Morgan Freeman). The owner of the saloon, who displays Ned's body in an open coffin as a warning to other bounty hunters, receives no forgiveness. Will Munny (Clint Eastwood) is himself unforgiven. In the past he has robbed and murdered men, women and children. It is said of him that he was the coldest, meanest, most unfeeling killer, even worse than Will Bonney (Billy the Kid). Those days, he tells Ned frequently, and especially late at night by a campfire, are now long over. He is not that way any more. The fact that he has to keep reiterating the fact suggests that he has not fully come to terms with his own past or forgiven himself.

The film opens with an idyllic scene: the ridge of a hill, a hut and tree in silhouette against an orange sky, somewhere in the middle of nowhere. A text on the screen tells us of a young woman who married a man of an 'intemperate disposition' and died here in 1878 of smallpox. Then we are in the town of Big Whiskey, Wyoming, in 1880. It is dark, there is heavy rain, a banjo is being played in a desultory fashion. A couple are copulating violently. Then follows the sequence which drives the rest of the plot. A prostitute makes a mild joke about the size of a man's organ and the man loses his temper and then all self-control, and stabs at her with a knife. He and his companion attempt to escape, leaving the woman mutilated, but they are caught. The sheriff, Little Bill, is called in. He will prove to be the most brutal and vicious of all the killers and would-be killers in the film. It becomes apparent that he has less concern for the law and justice than for his own authority. He does not want the world that he controls disturbed by interlopers. People are animals to him, livestock over which he has power. When the prostitutes cry for just punishment of the two indisputably guilty men, he at first considers beating them with a bullwhip, but then makes them pay fines, not in money but by giving a specified number of ponies to the 'owner' of the prostitutes, Skinny, by the following spring. The women are treated like property. Skinny actually brandishes a contract, 'proof of purchase', claiming they are his goods, and that the mutilated prostitute is in this sense 'damaged goods'. It makes perfect sense therefore to Little Bill that the cowboy who caused the injuries should pay five ponies and his companion two.

Although the cowboy did not kill the prostitute, it is impossible for her to continue working in her profession, so the other women pool their money to offer a reward for a killer to carry out revenge for them. This is the motor which drives the plot. Will is tempted because of his need to raise his two children and look after his run-down pig farm, but he is a changed man since he married. His now deceased wife was the person who helped him to give up his old ways – the murdering and drinking – for her and their children's sake.

Enter the Schofield Kid, a young man bent on killing the two men and getting the reward, and claiming to have killed five men already. Will never says as much then but it is clear that he doubts the boy's credentials, and says as much to Ned later in the film. Eventually Will changes his mind and follows the Kid, persuading his old gunfighter partner Ned to join him. There are several comically absurd elements in the film. Will has forgotten how to mount a horse properly and frequently falls off. The Schofield Kid turns out to be shortsighted and cannot see objects clearly beyond 50 yards. But the Kid serves a specific function in the story. He has sought Will out because of the legends that have spread about his character and prowess. The Kid wants to be like he imagines Will was in the past. The events of the film prove to be a painful learning process for him. He does succeed in killing one of the two men (Will kills the other), but then, after initial exhilaration, he is sickened to death by it and resolves to go home and give up his dream of being a gunfighter. Ned too gives up and attempts to go home when he realises that he can no longer kill a man. The stuff of legend may have once been reality but now only the legend remains.

Mr WW Beauchamp (Saul Rubinek) is the creator and disseminator of legends, and author of cheap novelettes, which retell the lives of infamous outlaws. Such men did indeed exist in nineteenth-century America. We meet Beauchamp in the company of English Bob (Richard Harris), a renowned bounty hunter, whose brief cameo appearance in the film also adds a further dimension. There is a law in Big Whiskey forbidding the carrying of firearms in the town, and English Bob flouts this law. Little Bill has heard of the offer of a reward by the prostitutes to attract bounty hunters and sees it as a threat to his authority. English Bob becomes one of his victims. Beauchamp is introduced as English Bob's biographer, and through the sheriff Beauchamp learns about the reality behind English Bob's reputation. A famous barroom shoot-out was in fact a rather botched affair, glorified in the retelling. This throws into doubt some of the reputations of many of the reputedly great gunslingers of the West. In his arrogant assertion of the superiority of a monarchy over a presidential system, English Bob presents a general criticism of the gun culture in America, in which it is possible to attempt to assassinate a president, while no one would dare threaten the majesty of royalty. On the day the confrontation between Little Bill and English Bob takes place, the flags are out on all the buildings, for it is Independence Day.

If Will can never fully forgive himself for his past actions (in his dreams he still sees some of his victims), he is now completely aware of the enormity of killing a man: 'It's a hell of a thing killing a man. You take away all he's got, and all he'll ever have'. And it seems that the Kid has come to a similar realisation early enough to save him: 'I can't kill nothing no more'.

In the final showdown when Will shoots Skinny and several other men, Beauchamp transfers his interest to Will. It is in awe that he says, 'You killed five men'. And it is perfectly in keeping with his character that among the last words of Little Bill, as he lies on the floor under Will's boot and facing his rifle, should be, 'I don't deserve to die like this…I was building a house'. The question is implied at the end: which of the two men is more brutalised, Will or Little Bill? They agree on what their fate will be in the hereafter. Little Bill says, 'I'll see you in hell William Munny', to which he receives the reply, 'Yeah!' before he is shot. But then Will has at least partly redeemed himself in his concern and affection for the mutilated prostitute. Were it not for his faithfulness to his wife's memory, they might have become lovers. We are told at the end in a postscript that he moved to San Francisco to bring up his children and set up a business. If his wife's mother could wonder why she married him, the audience at least has some inkling by the final credits. The dedication to 'Sergio and Don' (Sergio Leone and Don Siegel) indicates Clint Eastwood's debt to his experience in Leone's 'spaghetti westerns', but he has humanised his central character since those days, and given him a name…

RESOURCES

The following works were consulted during the writing of this book. All are recommended for the serious enthusiast. Some books are also included that cover fields which could be only be alluded to briefly here. A number of informative websites are also listed.

Brauer, R. and Brauer, D., *The Horse, the Gun, and the Piece of Property: Changing Images of the TV Western*, Ohio: Bowling Green University Popular Press, 1975.

Buscombe, Edward, *100 Westerns*, London: BFI, 2006. Perceptive analyses of selected westerns.

Cameron, . and Pye, D. (eds.), *The Movie Book of the Western*, London: Studio Vista, 1996.

Fagen, Herb, *The Encyclopaedia of Westerns*, New York: Checkmark Books, 2003. Alphabetical listings of over 3,500 films, with extensive appendices on the silent era and spaghetti westerns.

Frayling, C., *Spaghetti Westerns: Cowboys and Europeans from Karl May to Sergio Leone*, London & New York: Routledge and Kegan Paul/I.B.Tauris, 1998.

French, Philip, *Westerns: Aspects of a Movie Genre* and *Westerns Pevisited*, Manchester: Carcanet Press Ltd., 2005. This contains a useful review of recent books.

Kitses, Jim, *Horizons West*, London: BFI, 2004. Studies of major directors.

Lusted, David, *The Western*, Harlow UK: Pearson Education Ltd., 2003.

This contains an extensive bibliography.

Wyatt, E.M., (ed.) *'B' Western: Cowboys of the Silver Screen*, North Carolina: Raleigh Chapter of the Western Film Preservation Society.

WEBSITES

www.filmsite.org/westernfilm
Detailed essays on genres within the genre, e.g. silents, spaghetti westerns, etc.

www.questia.com/library/communication/film-genres.jsp
For serious studies and research on the genre.

www.simplyscripts.com/genre/western
For scripts of famous westerns.

www.wildeast.net/spaghettiwestern.htm
Colourfully illustrated site devoted to spaghetti westerns.

www.filmswildwest.com
Encyclopaedia of westerns.

INDEX

The index is restricted to the titles of westerns, directors, the well-known actors and a few others associated with the genre.